PMP® Examination Study Guide

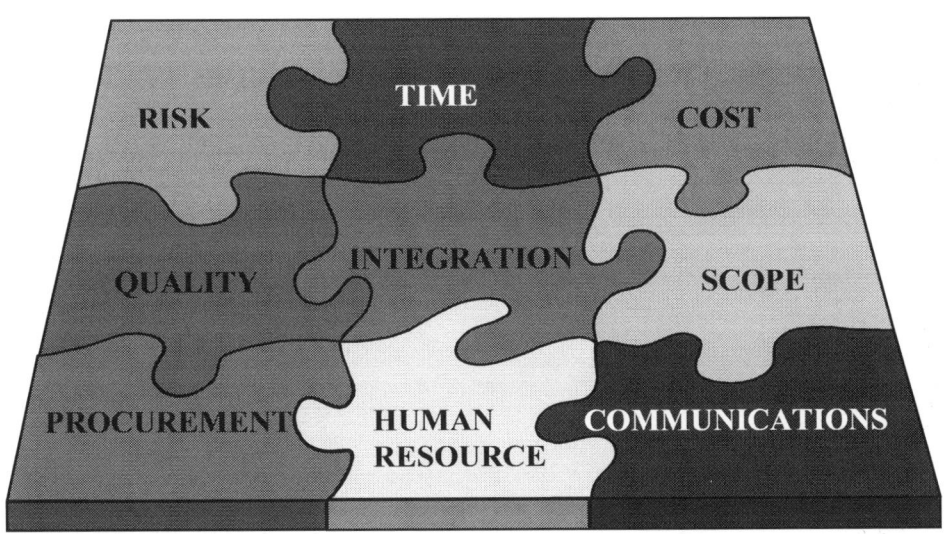

Revised PMBOK® Guide 4 edition

By Robin Kay BA MBA PMP

Changes from the previous edition

The major change is the addition to each chapter of answers to the practice questions with references to the text and further comment where required. In the previous edition there was simply a table of answers at the end of the book.

There have also been a number of minor changes, corrections and additions to the text.

Some questions have been modified whilst others have been removed and replaced.

ISBN: 978-1-4457-1167-6

Contents

David Crawford
420 Heysham Road, Heysham
Morecambe
Lancashire, LA3 2BL

Introduction

This introduction should be read carefully before commencing the Chapters. It contains important information

Course Objective & Target Audience

The objective of this book is to provide readers with sufficient information to pass the PMP examination. To this end it is not necessary to have attended any previous project management training, although PMI require applicants to show evidence of 35 hours training in some aspect of project management. Experience shows that the most successful candidates are those that have experience in a leadership capacity, in a projects environment and can relate that experience to the theory presented in this text.

PMI & *the PMBOK® Guide*

The Project Management Institution was established in 1969 and headquartered in the USA. PMI is the leading non-profit professional association in the area of Project Management, and currently supports over 100,000 members in 125 countries worldwide.

PMI members are individuals practicing and studying project management in many different industry areas, including aerospace, automotive, oil & gas, business management, construction, engineering, financial services, information technology, pharmaceuticals and telecommunications.

Over time, PMI has become, and continues to be, the leading professional association in project management. More information is available on the PMI website: - www.pmi.org

PMI is the publisher of *the PMBOK® Guide*. It is now in its fourth edition, and this course text has been revised in line with that version.

The primary purpose of the *PMBOK® Guide* is to identify and describe that subset of the Project Management Body of Knowledge that is generally accepted. Generally accepted means that the knowledge and practices described are applicable to most projects most of the time, and that there is widespread consensus about their value and usefulness.

The document is also intended to provide a common language within the profession and practice for talking and writing about project management. Project management is a relatively young profession, and while there is substantial commonality around what is done, there is relatively little commonality in the terms used. The PMBOK® provides a basic reference for anyone interested in the profession of project management. However it should be noted that the document is neither comprehensive nor all-inclusive.

The *PMBOK® Guide* Knowledge Areas

The *PMBOK® Guide* is organised under the following topics, known as Knowledge Areas

1 Project Integration Management
2 Project Scope Management
3 Project Time Management
4 Project Cost Management
5 Project Quality Management
6 Project Human Resource Management
7 Project Communications Management
8 Project Risk Management
9 Project Procurement Management

In addition there is a tenth topic known as Professional Responsibility

The Project Management Process Groups

Each Knowledge area consists of several processes and each process belongs to a particular process group. They are:-

- Initiating Processes
- Planning Processes
- Executing Processes
- Monitoring & Controlling Processes
- Closing Process

These 5 process groups are linked as follows:

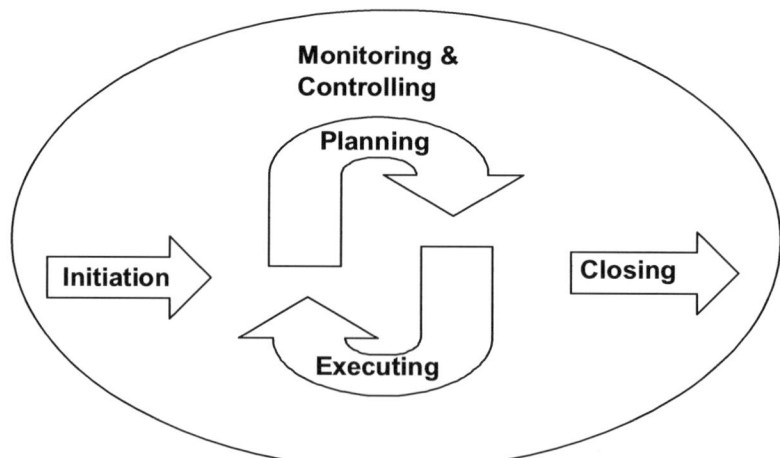

(Based on Figure 3-1. Project Management Process Groups - *PMBOK® Guide)*

Each of these process groups contains several processes. There are 42 in total and are listed in the table on page 18. Much of the *PMBOK® Guide* is devoted to detailing all the inputs and outputs of these processes. Note that this text does not attempt to describe in detail all the inputs and outputs for each process. This is covered more than adequately in the *PMBOK® Guide*

Some examination questions will refer to specific inputs and outputs of particular processes. Unless you have a photographic memory you should not attempt to memorise them all. In most instances an overall appreciation of *the PMBOK® Guide* will enable you to eliminate wrong answers and select the right one.

Examination Format

The PMP Certification Examination lasts 4 hours and is comprised of 200 four-option questions. There is one correct answer for each question. Although you are not aware of them, 25 of the question are "dummy questions". PMI put them in the exam to test their validity but they do not count towards your mark.

PMP Certification

Full details of PMP Certification including how and where to take the examination are explained in the PMP Handbook. It can be downloaded from the PMI website at www.pmi.org

Professional Development Units (PDUs)

In order to retain the PMP qualification evidence must be submitted, over a 3 year cycle, of professional development activities. PDUs can be collected in a variety of ways but the most common method is by ongoing training. Further information can be found in the PMP handbook and on the PMI website. www.pmi.org

Structure of the text

After an initial chapter covering some basic concepts, the text has a Chapter dedicated to each of the nine Knowledge Areas plus a tenth chapter covering Professional Responsibility. Each of these 10 chapters will be followed by practice examination questions of the type to be found in the exam.

Preparation for the exam

PMI recommend that preparation for the exam should include wide reading. However with this broad approach it is difficult to know where to draw the boundaries of study. This difficulty is compounded by the fact that PMI publish no "syllabus" for the exam. There is no prescribed list of books, which together form the total project management body of knowledge. The *PMBOK® Guide* describes each of the knowledge areas. However it is virtually impossible to pass the examination on the basis of studying just *the PMBOK® Guide*

The aim of this course is to complement the *PMBOK® Guide* so as to provide a concentrated source of revision material that reduces or eliminates the need for other material.

It is a feature of the PMI examination that a broad range of knowledge is more likely to generate a pass mark than detailed knowledge of more limited scope. In fact in many instances simply being aware of the existence of various tools and techniques and a broad understanding of how they can be applied is sufficient to answer the exam questions.

The Chapters that follow attempt to present revision material at a level necessary to pass the examination. The Chapters are not meant to be a comprehensive course in project management techniques and if a more in depth treatment is required on any topic then the appropriate textbooks should be consulted.

The *PMBOK® Guide* is an essential requirement for revision but no attempt should be made to study it in depth. In particular do not try to memorise all the processes and their inputs and outputs.

 It is recommended that *the PMBOK® Guide* is carefully read once all the way through and then only used for reference purposes.

After reading the *PMBOK® Guide* and studying the course material the best way of preparing for the exam is to get as much practice as possible at answering questions of the type likely to be asked in the exam. There are 360 sample questions in this text and many more free questions can be found on the Internet

Please bear in mind that unlike the Association of Project Management Exam, the PMP exam has no defined syllabus. Therefore it cannot be guaranteed that every question asked in the examination will be covered in this text, or any other text. In addition some questions will draw upon experience rather than knowledge.

Note also that PMI do not publish a pass mark. Each online examination is unique to each candidate with questions being randomly sampled from a large database. Each question has a difficulty rating associated with it and this information is used to generate a pass mark for each individual exam. As a rough guideline you should aim for consistently exceeding 75% in all your practice tests.

Chapter 1

Basic Project Concepts

1 Basic Project Concepts

This chapter attempts to clarify and simplify material that does not fit into any particular knowledge area but is necessary for an understanding of the entire project management process. It is based upon sections 1-3 of the *PMBOK® Guide*. However wherever it was thought appropriate, material has been covered in the knowledge area chapters. For instance Organisations have been covered in Human Resource Management

1.1 What is a Project?

Work done by any organisation generally comes under the heading of either Projects or Operations. They have the following in common:-

They are performed by people
They are constrained by finite resources
They involve Planning, Executing & Controlling

The PMI definition of a project is "A temporary endeavour, undertaken to provide a unique product or service. A project thus has the following additional attributes:-

1. It is temporary; e.g has a finite duration with a defined end point.
2. It is in some way unique.

Projects also exhibit the phenomena of Progressive Elaboration. Because the product of each particular project is unique it will undergo a process of progressive elaboration as the project proceeds. i.e. the final product will invariably improve in many incremental ways as understanding increases. This process must be carefully controlled. Note that change in Product Scope does not infer a change in Project Scope.

1.2 Program Management

Program Management is the co-ordinated management of a group of projects that are inter-related and/or interdependent and contribute to a common strategic objective.

Program Management is a strategic tool. Programs are generally overseen by the CEO and the Board.

Projects in a program can be in parallel or in series or a combination of both. Hence programs can be finite or ongoing.

Projects within a Program still have individual project managers who report to the program manager who in turn reports either to a senior sponsor who could be a board member or to the board itself.

1.3 Portfolio Management

There are two overlapping definitions of what we mean by a portfolio.

1) In a total business context a portfolio is defined as the totality of all an organisation's programs, projects and related operational activities.

2) A portfolio can also be described as a set of projects or programs that have no interdependencies and do not share a common objective. Projects may share resources but they are otherwise unconnected.

Portfolio management is particularly concerned with the management of resources across competing projects and   programs with particular regard to:-

- Scarce or limited resources and capacity bottlenecks
- Balance across the portfolio between risk and return
- Timing of the project i.e. when it takes place

Portfolio managers must ensure that senior management are provided with all the information they require in order to make appropriate decisions regarding the portfolio and will assist and influence them in making those decisions and making sure that the portfolio support the strategic direction of the organisation.

The relationship between project, program and portfolio management is illustrated in the figure below

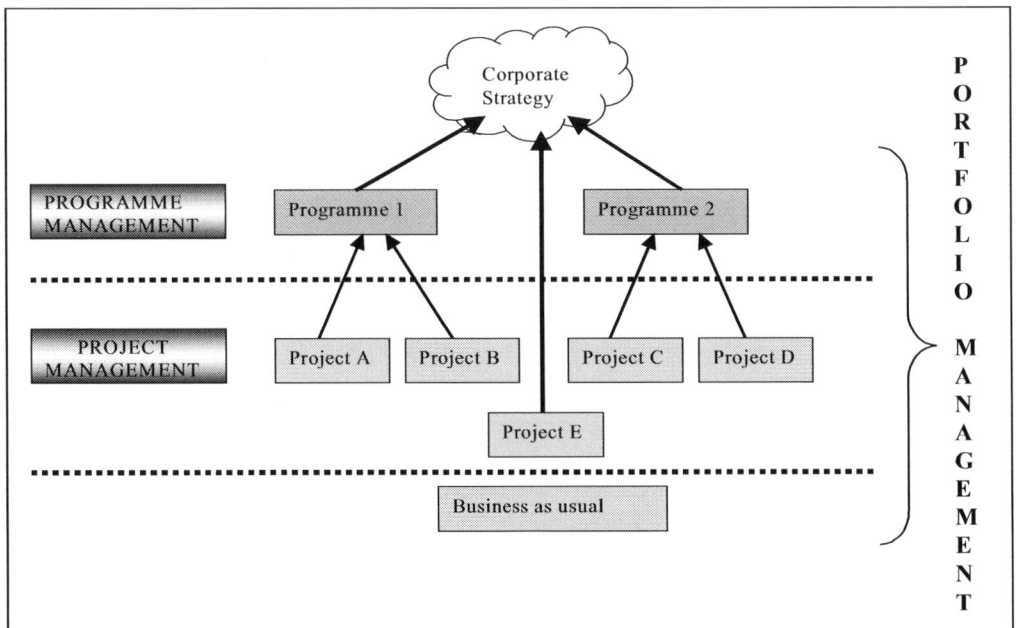

Relationship between project, program and portfolio management

1.4 Enterprise Environmental Factors

Projects do not take place in a vacuum. They take place within a "context" or "environment" and the successful accomplishment of a project generally requires a significant sensitivity to, and appreciation of, the context in which it is based. Note that the word Environment is not meant in the "Green" sense.

Some of these environmental factors are within the control of the project personnel but many are not. Many of them can significantly affect the project outcome hence they need to be monitored. They include elements that cover both the internal and external environment of the projects.

The project/program manager and the project sponsor share a responsibility for monitoring the project environment. In general terms the project manager would be primarily concerned with the internal environment and the sponsor with the external environment.

Examples of external factors are:

- Government and industry standards and regulations
- The competition
- National and global economic situation
- Supplier behaviour

Examples of internal factors are:

- Company methodology and organisation
- Company culture
- Company infrastructure and capability

1.5 Organisational Process Assets

Organisational Process Assets are listed as an input to many PMI processes. They consist simply of all the methods, standards, policies, procedures and rules that exist to guide and mandate project execution. Also included is the knowledge base of historical project files and lessons learned.

1.6 The Project Life Cycle

There are many different project lifecycles. Many companies define their own project life cycles and may have different life cycle models for different kinds of projects.

A common feature of all life cycles is the Gateway or Review process. At the end of each phase the project is subject to management review. The deliverables of each phase must be formally accepted before the project manager receives reconfirmation of his/her authority to continue the project.

What follows is a generic lifecycle that can represent just about any project.

The Phases can be remembered easily as CDEF.

Concept phase (or Initiation)

- Collect data
- Establish outline scope of project
- Define project objectives and overall strategy/justification
- Determine feasibility and possible risks
- Prepare Business Plan
- Estimate resources
- Develop project charter

Development (or Planning) phase

- Build the project team
- Develop scope baseline plan
- General Design
- Establish policies/procedures
- Prepare Outline Project Plan
- Identify and assess risks

Execution (or Implementation) phase

- Detailed Design
- Detailed Project Plan
- Set up and execute work packages
- Control Scope, Quality, Time, and Cost

Finishing (or Termination or Close-out) phase

- Acceptance
- Handover
- Post Project Review
- Archiving of records

The above is an example of a sequential relationship where one phase cannot commence until the previous one is complete. Some methodologies allow phases to overlap or even be iterative in nature. Such techniques can reduce overall project duration but can also substantially increase risk.

1.7 Product Life Cycle

It is important to differentiate between Project and Product life cycles.

A project usually results in the delivery of a finished product such as a building, an IT system, a road, a bridge etc. The project will have defined deliverables that will be accepted by the client or customer against a defined specification. At this point a handover takes place and after the closeout processes have been completed the **Project** life cycle is complete. However the Product life cycle carries on into Operation and eventually to Termination. This is illustrated overleaf.

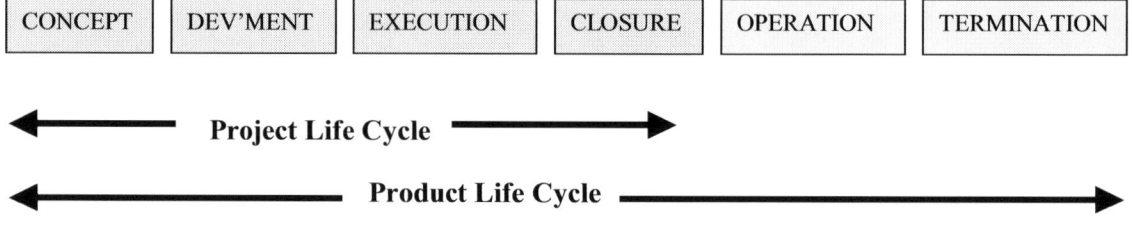

1.8 The Project Office

All organisations that take project management seriously will have a project office that exists to support the organisation's project needs. Major projects and/or programs may have their own dedicated support office. Where a project office does not exist the services must be provided from within the project.

At its simplest level the project office may just provide administrative support to project personnel. At the other extreme can become the "Centre of Excellence" for project management and the body to which project managers report. It will be the overseeing body for all project activity and be responsible for linking corporate strategy to project execution.

The Project Office can have various names depending on the organisation and the extent of its role e.g.

- PSO -Project Support Office
- PPSO-Projects and Programs Support Office
- PMO-Project Management Office
- EPMO-Enterprise Program Management Office

As a basic minimum a project office should provide the following functions:-

- Administrative support to project managers and team members
- Consolidation of individual project status reports into program and corporate reports including exception reporting
- Project process quality audit and assurance

Other possible functions are:-

- Identification and development of PM methodology, standards, documents, templates etc
- Co-ordination of resource allocation across all projects
- Selection, operation and management of project tools such as enterprise wide project management software
- Consolidation and dissemination of lessons learned
- Development and management of PM job descriptions and training programs and professional development.
- Organisation of mentoring and skills development
- Coordination of risk management initiatives across projects and programs
- Ensuring that individual project goals remain consistent with program and corporate goals

The presence of a project office allows an organisation to draw together its project management expertise, and makes possible the development of that expertise into a centre of excellence. A project management office fits particularly well with a strong matrix organisation (see page 136), as project managers and project office staff can be brought under common management. However for functional and weak/balanced structures some sort of project office is vital in order to facilitate a common approach to managing projects.

1.9 Governance

Corporate governance is the system by which companies are directed and controlled for the benefit of shareholders.

It provides:-

-
  - The structure through which organisational goals are set
  - The means by which the goals are to be met
  - The monitoring of performance against those goals

Boards of directors are responsible for the governance of their companies.

Project Governance is a subset of Corporate Governance and concerns those areas specifically related to project activities.

Effective Project Governance ensures:-

- The Project portfolio is aligned to Corporate goals

- Projects are delivered efficiently

- The Board and major stakeholders are provided with timely, relevant and accurate information

The effective Governance of project management will help ensure that the interests of directors, project staff, stockholders and other stakeholders are aligned and will reduce surprises.

Governance Principles

- Projects should be clearly linked to key business objectives
- There should be clear senior management ownership of project
- There should be effective engagement with stakeholders
- Leaders must have the required project and risk management skills
- There should be appropriate contact at senior level with key suppliers
- Projects should be driven by long term value rather than short term cost
- Projects should be broken down into manageable steps

1.10 Project Management Methodology

Many companies have a Project Methodology that consists of a collection of Policies Procedures, Guidelines, Templates and Mandatory Items, which together define how projects should be planned, monitored and controlled within an organisation. The adoption of PMI processes could be the basis of a methodology

The use of a Methodology has many advantages, the principal one being the provision of a consistent and structured approach across projects.

Benefits

- Make project handover easier with a common format between PM's
- Allow for roll-up of projects for a corporate viewpoint
- Encourages learning from project to project through a structured approach
- Fewer misunderstandings through using a common language
- A clear and consistent approach with agreed decision points along the way
- Fewer conflicts as clear roles and responsibilities are defined up front
- Effective communication between the various parties involved in the project
- Faster implementation time as less effort is spent reinventing the wheel each time
- Checklists for less experienced project managers reduces support needs
- Shows commitment from senior management to the implementation of projects.

1.11 Managing Project Success

Project Success Criteria

Defined as: "The qualitative or quantitative criteria by which the success of a project is judged".

Possible examples are:-

- Delivered within Time & Budget tolerance
- Delivered to Specification
- Customer Satisfaction rating achieved
- Health & Safety adhered to
- Business Benefits realised
- Increased market share
- Improved productivity

From the point of view of the Project Manager, success may be defined as delivering to time cost and specification. However other stakeholders may be more concerned with business benefits. These will probably not be known at time of handover. It is perfectly possible for a project to be deemed a delivery success but fail to produce its business benefits. On the other hand many projects delivered late and over budget have nevertheless delivered considerable business benefits. Ultimately, project success depends upon customer satisfaction.

Project Success Factors

Project Success Factors are those elements within the structure and context of the project that are conducive to success. These elements can be compared to *Hygiene Factors* (see page 147) in that their presence will not guarantee success but their absence will markedly increase the probability of failure.

Examples are:-

- Clear project mission
- Top management support
- Client consultation
- Committed project personnel
- Monitoring and feedback mechanisms
- Clear communications
- Adequate resources

Key Performance Indicators

Key Performance Indicators are continuously measured over the life of the project. They directly measure the project performance against Project Success Criteria. Although success criteria can be qualitative or quantitative ideally they should be SMART. i.e.

- Specific
- Measurable
- Accountable
- Realistic
- Timely

1.12 Project Management Processes

The PMI approach to project management is based upon the concept of project management processes. In the words of the *PMBOK® Guide* "A process is a set of interrelated actions and activities performed to achieve a pre-specified product, result or service".

This is illustrated below.

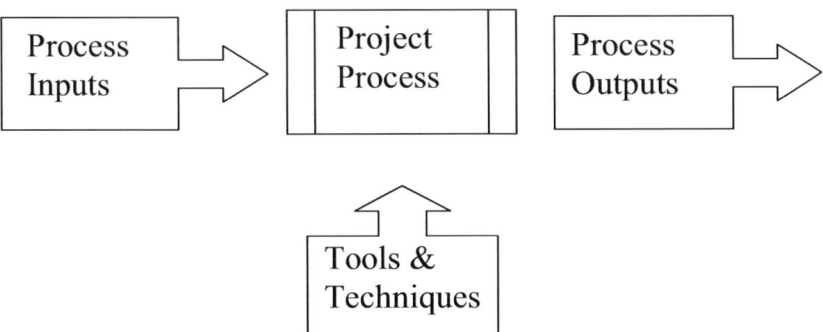

The *PMBOK® Guide* defines 42 project management processes. The Processes are organised into 5 categories known as Process Groups.

Knowledge Areas	Process Groups				
	Initiation	Planning	Executing	Monitor & Control	Closing
Project Integration Management	1 Develop Project Charter	2 Develop Project Management Plan	3 Direct & Manage Project Execution	4 Monitor & Control Project Work 5 Perform Integrated Change Control	6 Close Project or Phase
Project Scope Management		1 Collect Requirements 2 Define Scope 3 Create WBS		4 Verify Scope 5 Control Scope	
Project Time Management		1 Define Activities 2 Sequence Activ's 3 Estimate Activity Resources 4 Estimate Activity Durations 5 Develop Schdule		6 Control Schedule	
Project Cost Management		1 Estimate Costs 2 Determine Budget		3 Control Costs	
Project Quality Management		1 Plan Quality	2 Perform Quality Assurance	3 Perform Quality Control	
Project Human Resource Management		1 Develop Human Resource Plan	2 Acquire Project Team 3 Develop Project Team 4 Manage Project Team		
Project Communications Management	1 Identify Stakeholders	2 Plan Communications	3 Distribute Information 4 Manage Project Stakeholders	5 Report Performance	
Project Risk Management		1 Plan Risk Management 2 Identify Risks 3 Perform Qualitative Risk Analysis 4 Perform Quantative Risk Analysis 5 Plan Risk Responses		6 Monitor & Control Risks	
Project Procurement Management		1 Plan Procurements	2 Conduct Procurements	3 Administer Procurements	4 Close Procurements

The bulk of the *PMBOK® Guide* (chapters 4-12) is concerned with describing the 42 processes within the context of the 9 Knowledge Areas. The *PMBOK® Guide* also lists the tools and techniques applicable to each process. A large part of the PMP exam is concerned with knowledge of these tools and techniques. However the *PMBOK® Guide* is mainly concerned with processes and the PMP examination requires knowledge of tools and techniques beyond the scope of the *PMBOK® Guide*.

Thus much of this volume is concerned with providing descriptions of tools and techniques at a level appropriate to the examination.

Although processes are described as individual entities it must be recognised that they are overlapping activities that can be repeated throughout the project. Outputs from one process will provide inputs to others and the interactions can be very complex.

It should also be noted that not every process is relevant to every project and it is the responsibility of the project manager to decide which processes are appropriate.

Chapter 2

Project Integration Management

1 Project Integration Management Processes

1.1 Develop Project Charter

The document that formally authorises a project

1.2 Develop Project Management Plan

The document that defines how the project will be planned and managed

1.3 Direct and Manage Project Execution

How the work of the work of the project is to be carried out.

1.4 Monitor and Control Project Work

The means by which it is ensured that the project plan is followed

1.5 Perform Integrated Change Control

The management and control of change requests.

1.6 Close Project or Phase

Describes the activities required to formally close the project.

(Note the Preliminary Scope Statement in the *PMBOK® Guide* 3rd edition has been removed)

2 Develop Project Charter

You need to be familiar with what a project charter is.

The project charter formally recognises the existence of the project and describes the project objectives and deliverables and the business need it is addressing. It is the document that provides the project manager with formal approval to execute the project.

It should include:

- High level statement of project purpose and objectives
- High level requirements
- Project success criteria
- Summary milestone schedule
- Stakeholder influences
- Summary budget
- Assigned PM and authority level

The Project Charter is created during the concept phase of a project. It is normally the responsibility of the sponsoring management to create the charter even though in practice the task is often delegated to the project manager. For projects carried out under a formal contract then the contract itself can form the project charter or can be an input to it.

2.1 Business Case

The Business Case is the primary input to the Project Charter. The objective in developing a Business Case is to provide a justification for carrying out the project. It must show the expected costs and benefits of the project and how it fits in with the company strategy and contributes to the corporate goals of the organisation. Not all costs and benefits are tangible, i.e. they cannot easily be expressed in purely monetary terms.

In any organisation there are usually many proposed projects that are competing for limited funds. Therefore the purpose of the Business Case is not just to demonstrate why a project is viable in its own right but also why it should be favoured over others.

The Business Case is prepared very early in the project life cycle. As normally no detailed planning has taken place it is often difficult to decide the level of detail in the Business Plan. The answer is that it should contain enough information to enable a decision to be made as to whether to carry on with the project. The decision can always be modified in the light of more detailed planning. Typical contents are as follows

- Description of Problem/Opportunity and Scope outline
- Other options (including do nothing)
- Principal reason for carrying it out
- Project Deliverables/Objectives
- Fit to the organisation's business strategy
- Emphasis on Time/Cost/Quality
- Outline Schedule and Major Milestones
- Investments Appraisal
- Source of funds
- Expected Costs & Benefits-Both tangible and intangible
- High Level Risks
- Success Criteria
- Assumptions
- Stakeholder Analysis
- Impact on Business as Usual

2.2 Project selection methods

The creation of a project charter presupposes that a project has been selected and justified in a business plan. Such justification involves measuring and comparing the costs and benefits of the project. Any or all of the following tools can be used.

- Benefit-cost models/ Economic models (see Cost Management, Chapter 5)
- Peer review/Expert opinion
- Scoring models/Checklists (See figure overleaf)
- Payback (see Cost Management)
- Present Value/DCF/IRR (see Cost Management)

Below is an example of a scoring model. Each individual project is given a score for each category. This information can then be used to prioritise the projects.

	1	2	3	4	5
Estimated Revenue					
Production Costs					
R&D Costs					
Level of Risk					
Payback Period					
Strategic Fit					
Etc……					

KEY
1 Unacceptable
2 Unfavourable
3 Acceptable
4 Favourable
5 Very favourable

2.3 Tools & Techniques

The *PMBOK® Guide* lists no formal tools for creating the Project Charter. The only technique is that of Expert Judgement which can come from many sources both internal and external to the company.

3 Develop Project Management Plan

The primary purpose of project plan development is to create a document to guide project execution and control. The most important inputs to the Project Management Plan are the Project Charter and the Project Scope Statement (See Chapter 3). There may also be constraints such as resources and budget.

3.1 Project Plan Content

All of the following items are normally contained within the Project Plan although some may on occasions be separate subsidiary documents, which are referenced by the project plan. Each section or subsidiary plan is detailed to the extent required by the specific project.

- Project Charter
- Objectives and Deliverables
- Constraints and Assumptions
- Processes, tools and technique to be used
- Work Breakdown Structure
- Schedule
- Major Milestones
- Resource and Organisation Plan
- Roles and Responsibilities
- Performance Measurements
- Risk Analysis
- Change & Configuration Management Plan
- Budget and Cash Flow
- Quality Plan
- Communications Plan
- Procurement Plan
- Stakeholder Management Plan

Project Management Plan content will vary according to who is to see it. e.g. there may be a client version and an internal version.

The Project Management Plan is a live, configuration controlled document that builds upon the information contained in the Business Plan. It provides a contract between the Sponsor and the Project Manager. It is a reference point for reviews, audits and control. It also assists effective handover in the event of a change in project management or sponsorship. It is the primary tool for Stakeholder communication. The recipients are defined in the Communications Management Plan. (Chapter 8 para 3.1)

3.2 Project Plan Development

Here again the only Tool/Technique specified by the *PMBOK® Guide* is Expert Judgement.

There are many possible sources of input for project plan development but they all come down to answering 7 fundamental questions:-

1. **Why are you doing this project?**

   This is developed in the Business Case. It describes the need or problem being addressed and why it is necessary to do so.

2. **What are you trying to achieve?**

   This describes the scope of the project in terms of what exactly what is to be delivered. It will also describe the success criteria and the key performance indicators.

3. **How are you going to do it?**

   This describes the project strategy including the tools and techniques to be used, the monitoring and controlling processes and reporting arrangements. It will also cover fundamental decisions such as choice of methodology, life cycle and use of third parties.

4. **Who are the human resources needed?**

   This describes project roles and responsibilities, organisational structures and plans for human resource acquisition.

5. **When do you plan to do it by?**

   This documents the project schedule including key milestones.

6. **Where will the work take place?**

   This describes the geographical locations where the work will be carried out

7. **How much will it cost?**

    This costs all the project resource requirements including manpower costs, materials and equipment and states the project budget with expected spending by time period and by phase.

Although the project manager is responsible for seeing that the project plan is developed, the entire project team must contribute to it. For a project plan to be successful the whole project team must "buy in" to it. The plan must also have the agreement of major stakeholders so their input is also important.

4 Direct and Manage Project Execution

This is all about the multiple and interrelated actions that the Project Manager and team need to execute in order to accomplish the work detailed in the project plan.

Examples are:
- Obtain, organise, train, manage and motivate project team members
- Obtain bids, offers quotations etc
- Select suppliers and contractors
- Create, verify and validate project deliverables
- Manage Risk
- Manage suppliers and contractors
- Manage change
- Collect performance data
- Manage communication and reporting

These topics will be covered in the chapters to follow.

5 Monitor and Control Project Work

Monitoring and Controlling processes must be in place to:-
1. Ensure that human and physical resources are available when needed
2. Avoid unplanned increases in the scope of work.
3. Ensure that deviations for the plan are quickly identified so that remedial action can be taken.

As soon as Project Execution starts it must be continuously monitored until project completion.
The Baseline for monitoring and controlling the work of the project is the Project Management Plan.
It is used to :-

- Document planning assumptions
- Document planning decisions
- Facilitate communication among stakeholders

- Define review points
- Document roles and responsibilities

…..but most importantly, to provide a baseline for measuring and controlling progress.

Monitoring and Control is essentially a closed loop process where plan deviations are picked up by the monitoring processes and give rise to corrective actions which feed back into project execution.

The following tools may be used.

5.1 Earned Value Analysis

A key tool for monitoring and controlling projects is Earned Value. This will be covered in detail in the chapter 4.

5.2 Project Management Information Systems (PMIS)

A PMIS consists of all the tools, procedures and processes necessary to collect, collate and disseminate the information generated as an outcome of the project management processes. It should include integrated tools for schedule control, configuration management, information collection and distribution and document management and control

It is a key tool for project monitoring and control. Also referred to as **Information Management.**

6. Integrated Change Control

6.1 Change Control is concerned with:

- Influencing the factors which create change
- Determining that change has occurred
- Managing the actual changes that occur

It requires:

- Maintaining the integrity of performance measurement baselines.
- Ensuring that changes to product scope are reflected in the definition of the product.
- Coordinating the changes across all knowledge areas (affect of change on scope, cost, risk, quality, resources etc.)

It has a contractual orientation.

- Makes sure you do exactly what you said you would do.
- Protects project staff from unauthorised change requests
- Strictly defines the system deliverables
- Rigorously controls changes to the deliverable

- Ensures that what is delivered is consistent with the system as originally designed with modifications as per approved changes

The only tools and techniques are Expert Judgement and Change Control Meetings.

6.2 The Change Control Board (CCB)

Large projects should always have a formal change control board to approve or deny formal change requests. For smaller projects this may be an unacceptable overhead and decisions may be made by the Client/Sponsor or appropriate Stakeholders or by the PM. The CCB or Sponsor may delegate responsibility for approving some changes but they must still go through the same formal process.

6.3 Key Documents:-

Change Request Form:- A document for formally requesting a change, recording the impact and the decision of the Change Control Board. Change requests must always be made formally in writing.

Change Log:- Records all change requests and keeps track of status

There are three basic objectives of any change management system:

a) To screen user requests

- Use a change request form addressed to the project manager
- Evaluate the impact of the requested changes.
- If the impact is minimal the project manager can accept it. Otherwise, it should be escalated to the CCB. (Change Control Board)

b) To keep track of agreed changes

- Maintain a change log of all change requests and their status
- Update specifications where necessary

c) To update all baselines within the Project Management Plan and inform project staff of changes.

6.4 Sources of Change Requests

Changes can arise from 3 main areas:-

1. From errors and omissions in the original planning.
2. From evolution of project requirements or new techniques
3. Legal/mandatory changes

Anyone can ask for a change but all requests must be via the formal system and must be in writing although in an emergency some approvals can be automatic.

6.5 Configuration Management

Configuration Management is the processes and procedures to support Integrated Change Control. Its prime purpose is to manage and control the product configuration and changes to product scope. It must ensure that the system integrity is maintained when changes are made to individual configuration items and that a full audit chain of all changes is maintained.

Configuration control relates not just to project products but to all controlled items including plans, designs, product specifications, test specifications etc.

The configuration management system maintains the status of each individual configuration item. It shows the dependencies between configuration items and their version history. Each configuration item is specified in terms of its functional and physical characteristics and its dependencies on other items.

The Configuration Management System must be totally aligned with the Change Control System. Its ability to identify possible knock on effects will facilitate change assessment and will also protect different versions of the deliverable.

Configuration Management is not just a project tool but is a key tool in the subsequent operation and maintenance of the project deliverables.

Configuration management consists of 5 principal activities:-

1. **Configuration Management Planning**
   Establishes project specific procedures and defines tools, roles and responsibilities

2. **Configuration Identification**
   Breaking down the project deliverables into individual configuration items and creating a unique numbering system.

3. **Configuration Control**
   Maintains version control of all configuration items and the interrelationship between items.

4. **Configuration Status Accounting**
   Recording of all events that have happened to a system under development to allow comparison with the development plan and to provide traceability.

5. **Configuration Audit**

   Carried out to demonstrate that the products produced conform to the current specification and all procedures have been followed

The following diagram shows the change control process and its interaction with configuration management.

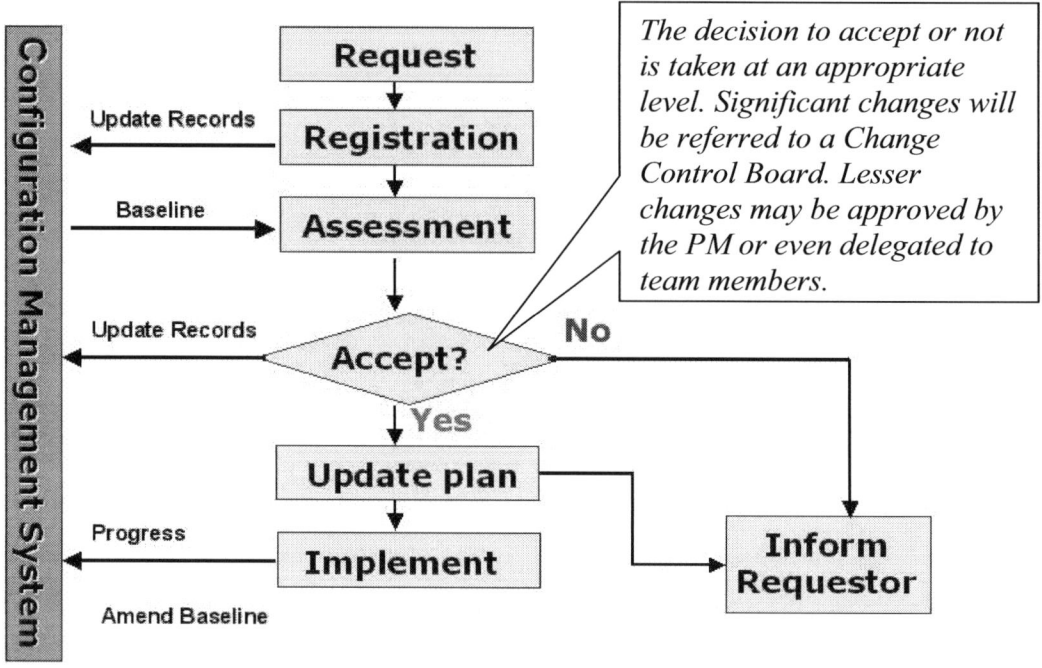

7 Close Project or Phase

It is important that projects and phases are formally closed down. Although most closure processes relate to the final project closure it is also necessary to make sure that phases are formally closed, by ensuring that all specified exit criteria have been met. Note that not all projects proceed to completion. Some projects may be terminated prematurely but it is still important to properly close the project down.

The following is a list of project closedown activities, some of which are also applicable to phase closure.

Handover of Deliverables

- Formal handover of product/facility
- Maintenance procedures - Training
- Definition and resolution of snagging lists
- Handover must be formal and recorded to ensure handing over of responsibilities

Admin Closeout

- Tidying up and archiving of project files
- Client documentation
- Completion of audit trail
- Disposal of surplus stocks & equipment

Contract Completion
- Formal acceptance
- Payments received
- Subcontractors paid

Financial Accounting
- All costs and revenues reconciled to baseline budget and any changes

Prepare for the post-project review
- The primary purpose of the post project review is to record lessons learned so that they can be used to improve the performance of future projects
- It should be chaired by an independent facilitator

Hold a close-out meeting
- Takes place with the client/customer to ensure there are no outstanding issues and formally close down the project

Conduct Post Project Review
- Formal review of the management of the project to document lessons learned

Staff Issues
- Re-deployment
- Feedback on performance
- Exit plan to complete outstanding tasks.

8 Benefits Review

This review takes place some time after project closure after sufficient time has elapsed to demonstrate the performance of the project deliverables. It is meant to show whether or not the benefits claimed in the Business Case have materialised. It is the responsibility of the project sponsor. After acceptance and handover the project manager normally has no further responsibility. However all projects managers should always have in mind the expected project benefits and take actions accordingly to maximise the chance of achieving them.

Integration Management Practice Questions

1. The primary purpose of project plan development is to—

   a   Create a document to guide project execution and control
   b   Document project assumptions and constraints
   c   Promote communication among stakeholders
   d   Define key project reports

2. Overall change control is primarily concerned with—

   a   Influencing factors that cause change, determining that change has occurred, and managing actual changes as they occur
   b   Maintaining integrity of baselines, integrating product and project scope, and coordinating change across knowledge areas
   c   Integrating deliverables from different functional specialties on the project
   d   Establishing a change control board that oversees the overall changes on the project

3. Which of the following regarding change requests is untrue?

   a   Any person can submit a change request
   b   They can be legally mandated
   c   They can be submitted orally to the project manager
   d   They can be externally or internally initiated

4. Which of the following is not an example of a project success factor?

   a   Top Management Support
   b   Delivering to Time and Budget
   c   A Clear Project Mission
   d   Adequate Resources

5. Which of the following would you not expect to find in the Project Charter?

   a   Project success criteria
   b   Outline budget and schedule
   c   Project Manager authority level
   d   Project team roles & responsibilities

6. All approved changes should be reflected in the—

   a   Performance report
   b   Change management plan
   c   Quality assurance plan
   d   Project management plan

7. Of the following, which is not always true of Programs and Program Management?

a   Programs are usually strategic
b   Programs are finite
c   All projects in a program are interdependent
d   Program managers usually report to a senior executive

8. Which of the following is not part of Direct and Manage Project Execution?

a   Manage expected project benefits
b   Manage risk
c   Manage change
d   Manage contractors

9. Portfolio Management is:

a   The co-ordinated management of a group of projects that are inter-related and/or
      interdependent and contribute to a common strategic objective.
b   The totality of all an organisation's programs, projects and related operational activities.
c   A set of projects or programs that have no interdependencies and no common objective.
d   Either B or C

10. Overall change control system is concerned with three major factors.
Which one is not a factor?

a   Influencing factors which create change
b   Determining that change has occurred
c   Reporting the changes
d   Managing the changes

11. Although an output of the various control processes, corrective action is also an input to
project plan execution because it—

a   Ensures that project objectives are met
b   Expedites actions to ensure that activities are completed on time
c   Completes the feedback loop needed to ensure effective project management
d   Involves performing a planned response for a specific project risk event

12. A project management information system comprises—

a   The project management software used for schedule development
b   All the required reports to be prepared on the project, who receives each one, and the method
      of distribution
c   The policies and procedures to follow as the project is performed
d   The tools and techniques used to gather, integrate, and disseminate the output of the other
      project management processes

13. A change control board is—

a. Recommended for use on all projects, large or small
b. Used as required to approve or reject change requests
c. Managed by the project manager who serves as its secretary
d. Composed of key members of the project team

14. The project plan should be distributed to—

a   All stakeholders in the performing organization
b   All project stakeholders
c   Project team members and the project sponsor
d   Those people defined in the communication management plan

15. Configuration management is any documented procedure used to apply technical and administrative direction and surveillance to:

a   Control any changes to the functional and physical characteristics of an item or system
b   Maintain an objective measurement of project implementation status
c   Make sure senior management is kept in the loop
d   Define performance objectives for earned value

16. The change control system includes—

a   Procedures to define how documents may be changed
b   Specific change requests expected on the project and plans to respond to each one
c   Performance reports that forecast project changes
d   A description of the functional and physical characteristics of an item or system

17. Typically, change control systems include automatic approval of certain types of changes. An example of such a change is one that is—

a   Suggested by the project sponsor
b   The result of an emergency
c   Suggested by the customer
d   Made mandatory by a new regulation

18. Within the 5 process groups which process is superimposed on the other 4?

a   Planning
b   Monitoring & Control
c   Execution
d   Closure

19. **Which of the following would you not expect to find in a business case.**

a   Investment appraisal
b   Detailed budget
c   Stakeholder analysis
d   Milestone Plan

20. **Which of the following tasks is not performed in configuration management?**

a   Identifying functional and physical characteristics of an item or system
b   Revising the schedule as the configuration changes
c   Performing an audit to verify conformance to requirements
d   Allowing automatic approval of some changes

21. **As applied to projects, temporary means that—**

a   Projects are short in duration
b   Every project has a definite beginning and end
c   The undertaking will end at an undetermined time in the future
d   Projects can be cancelled at any time

22. **Who should contribute to the development of the project plan?**

a   Project manager
b   All team members and stakeholders
c   Senior management
d   The project manager assisted by appropriate team members and stakeholders

23. **Which of the following is an example of a constraint in project plan development?**

a   Records of past performance
b   Financial reports from similar projects
c   A predefined budget
d   Lessons learned from prior projects

24. **Performance measurement techniques are useful in overall change control because they—**

a   Help show the status of the project
b   Measure overall project progress
c   Summarize information on the project for reporting to stakeholders
d   Help assess whether variances from the plan require corrective action

25. The primary purpose of a project planning methodology is to—

a   Provide a structured approach to guide the project team in project plan development
b   Ensure that all required forms are completed
c   Ensure that organizational policies and procedures are followed during the development and execution of the project plan
d   Serve as a repository of lessons learned that can be applied to the current project

26. Lessons learned from projects are significant because they—

a   Must be collected to meet requirements of organizational policies and procedures
b   Show the causes of variances and the reasons certain corrective actions were selected
c   Show why certain projects were selected by the organization over others
d   Show why certain people were selected as project manager and team members over others.

27. Which of the following is not a governance principle?

a   Project managers should be suitably experienced and be formally qualified.
b   Projects must be aligned to key business goals
c   Projects should be driven by long term value
d   There should be effective stakeholder management

28. Which of the following is not a project success factor?

a   Clear project mission
b   Client consultation
c   Business benefits realised
d   Adequate resources

29. Which of the following would you not normally expect to find in a project management plan?

a   Expected cash flow
b   Work Breakdown Structure
c   Source of project funding
d   Change Management Plan

30. Which of the following is not an Enterprise Environmental Factor?

a   Weather conditions
b   Government and industry standards and regulations
c   The competition
d   National and global economic situation

31. Which of the following is not part of the project plan?

a   The project charter
b   The WBS
c   Performance measurement baselines for schedule and cost
d   The project team members' remuneration plan

32. Controlling occurs—

a   On a continual basis throughout the project
b   At the end of each phase of the project life cycle to assess its success in meeting project objectives
c   At the end of each planning process
d   On a continual basis throughout the executing process and as needed in the other processes

33. Which of the following does not define a project life cycle?

a   Concept, Planning, Execution, Finishing
b   Initiation, Planning, Implementation, Termination
c   Concept, Development, Implementation, Close-out
d   Initiation, Planning, Execution, Operation, Termination

34. Which of the following is the most important reason for revising the project plan?

a   A Supplier has changed the product specification
b   The schedule has been crashed to meet the end dates
c   A key resource has been lost
d   The project sponsor has changed

35. Within the 5 process groups which processes are considered to be most vital:

a   Initiating
b   Monitoring & Controlling
c   Planning and Executing
d   All are equally important

36. Which of the following is not one of the three basic objectives of a change management system?

a   To screen change requests
b   To track agreed changes
c   To update plans and specifications
d   To minimise change to the project

PRACTICE QUESTION ANSWERS

		Page	Paragraph	
1	A	24	3	
2	A	27	6.1	
3	C	28	6.4	
4	B	17	1.11	B) is a Project Success *Criteria*
5	D	22	2	D) is too detailed a requirement at this stage
6	D	28	6.3c	
7	B	10	1.2	Programs can be ongoing as new projects are added
8	A	26	4	Project benefits do not normally arise until after project completion
9	D	11	1.3	
10	C	27	6.1	
11	C	26	5	
12	D	27	5.2	
13	B	28	6.2	Some change requests may not be significant enough to justify a CCB review
14	D	25	3.1	
15	A	29	6.5	
16	A	27	6.1	Changes to documents are controlled in the same way as physical items
17	B	28	6.4	
18	B	6		
19	B	23	2.1	A Business Case is normally made before detailed planning has taken place
20	D	28	6.4	
21	B	10	1.1	
22	D	26	3.2	
23	C	24	3	
24	D	27	6	Performance measurement helps in determining if change has occurred
25	A	16	1.10	
26	B	46	6.5	
27	A	15	1.9	Project managers must have appropriate skills but there is no requirement for formal qualifications.
28	C	17	1.11	Realising business benefits is a success criteria not a success factor
29	C	24	3.1	Source of project funding would be addresses in the Business Case
30	A	12	1.4	
31	D	24	3.1	
32	A	26	5	
33	D	13	1.6,1.7	Operation is part of the Product life cycle
34	B	65	3.10	Crashing involves shortening the schedule hence re-planning is required.
35	D	6		
36	D	28	6.3	Although it is desirable to minimise changes that is not an objective of the process

Chapter 3

Project Scope Management

1 Scope Management Processes

Scope Management is concerned with the processes required to ensure that the project includes ALL the work required and ONLY the work required, in order to complete the project successfully.

PMI views Scope Management as a 5 step process.

1.1 Collect Requirements

Consists of collecting and documenting Stakeholder requirements in terms of the required functionality of the project deliverables

1.2 Define Scope

The process of developing a written scope statement that defines the scope of the project and the project deliverables.

1.3 Create Work Breakdown Structure (WBS)

Defined as the process of breaking down the project deliverables (as identified in the Scope Statement) into smaller, more manageable components.

1.4 Verify Scope

The process of formally accepting the project deliverables by verifying that they conform to the agreed requirements.

1.5 Control Scope

Influencing the factors that create scope changes and controlling their impact and ensuring that all changes are processed through the Integrated Change Control Process. (Page 27)

Be aware that Scope Management encompasses both Project Scope and Product Scope.

2 Collect Requirements

A Requirements Specification is a statement, in a natural language, of what user services the system is expected to provide. It should be written so that it is understandable by the client and contractor management and by potential users. In order to correctly scope the project it is obviously of vital importance that correct requirements are obtained. However it is a common feature of SW projects in particular that what is delivered is often not what is required.

One of the best ways to ensure the quality of any project is to get the requirements for it right. If the requirements are not clearly and completely set out, any project or design based on them cannot succeed. Getting the requirements right at an early stage will prevent escalation of costs due to rework, client dissatisfaction and excessive changes during project execution and subsequent maintenance.

Requirements are about what is required and not about how they will be achieved. During the Concept phase high level requirements are gathered and they will be subsequently developed and revised during the Definition phase and beyond.

2.1 The Requirements Process

The requirements are the foundation on which the project is built so it is essential that they be gathered in a controlled and formal manner. This is essentially a four step process:-

1 Capture

Requirements are captured mainly by interviewing relevant stakeholders. It is necessary to gain a wide spectrum of opinions to make sure that all possible requirements are captured.

2 Analysis

The gathered requirements must be tested for feasibility, validity, compatibility, acceptability, applicability and consistency. It is often found that some of the requirements of different stakeholders are mutually exclusive or are very difficult to provide. All such issues must be cleared before finalising the requirements. If necessary the Sponsor must act as referee.

3 Prioritisation

It is often not possible to include all the requirements into time and budget constraints. It is therefore usual to prioritise the requirements and exclude some of them from the project scope. Here again the Sponsor may have to referee.

4 Acceptance Test Development

Once the requirements have been agreed acceptance rests must be devised and agreed. They are best done at this stage rather than at completion because they clarify understanding of the requirements and will often cause them to be modified. Acceptance tests are best devised by potential end users under the guidance of the project team.

2.2 Tools & Techniques

PMI suggest several tools and techniques to assist with the above process.

- Interviewing stakeholders individually
- Bringing stakeholders together in a Focus Group or Facilitated Workshop
- Carrying out surveys and questionnaires
- Observing people in their workplace
- Building prototypes to generate feedback

2.3 Stakeholder Requirements Documentation

The primary output of the above process is a document that describes the individual requirements and how they address the business needs of the organisation. This is often referred to as **The Functional Specification.** This document captures all the agreed user requirements in an unambiguous manner. It defines *what* is required but not *how* the requirement will be met. As its name implies it describes the functions of the system.

Requirements typically evolve over the life of a project. (*This is sometimes called Progressive Elaboration*) The Functional Specification is therefore a living document that is subject to *Change Control* and *Configuration Management.*

Each defined function will have an appropriate acceptance test for that function.
The Functional Specification will also specify appropriate quality parameters e.g performance requirements.

The way that each requirement links to a business need can be represented by a **Requirements Traceability Matrix.** Such a tool can also record the origin, rationale and evolving status of each requirement.

3 Define Scope

This process takes as its primary inputs the **Project Charter** and the **Stakeholder Requirements Documentation**

The output of this process is the **Project Scope Statement**

Once created the Project Scope Statement is a component of the Project Management Plan. Its level of detail is consistent with the needs of the project.

As its name implies the Scope Statement defines the overall scope of the project and ensure a common understanding of the scope amongst all the stakeholders. It must detail the following:-

- Project objectives
- Project boundaries
- Deliverables and specifications
- Acceptance criteria
- Constraints
- Assumptions

4 Create Work Breakdown Structure

The project work breakdown structure (WBS) is the framework on which the project is built. It is not possible to build a realistic project plan without first developing a WBS that details all the project tasks that must be accomplished. The process of creating the WBS causes the project manager and all involved with the planning process to carefully consider all aspects of the project.

A WBS breaks down a project into its component parts and provides a graphic picture of the hierarchy of the project. It progresses level by level first into sub projects or phases then to activities and finally into tasks. As the levels become lower, the scope, complexity, and cost of each element become smaller, until individual Work Packages are reached. Work Packages are manageable units of work that can be planned, budgeted, scheduled, and controlled as individual entities. This process is known as **decomposition**. The WBS shows how each work package contributes to the overall project objectives and so provides a firm basis for both planning and controlling the project.

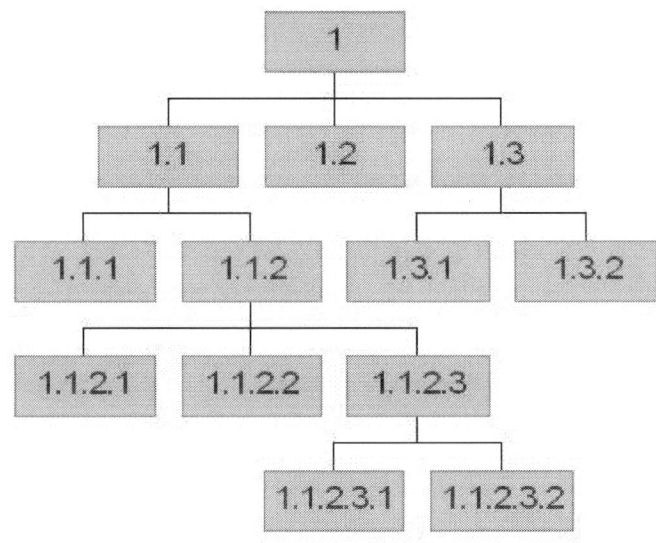

The size of these Work Packages is very important because they must be small enough to allow realistic estimates to be made, but also not so small so that the sheer number of tasks overwhelms the planning and control process. A useful rule of thumb is the *80 hour rule*. This states that a work package should generally be no more than 80 hours effort.

For higher level management reporting and control, or where lower level detail is not yet available, **control points** can be placed at selected points above the work package. For example item 1.1.2 above could be a **control point**. (Sometimes called cost centres).

In addition work packages below the control points can be grouped into **planning packages**. 1.1.2.3 could be a planning package.

4.1 WBS dictionary

Each component of the WBS is allocated a unique reference number known as the **code of accounts.** The information relating to each component is documented in the WBS dictionary. Typical content would be:-

- Statement of work
- Planned duration
- Budget
- Responsibility
- Resource requirements
- Specification
- Acceptance criteria
- Contract information
- Dependencies

4.2 Principal Benefits of using a WBS

- Its production facilitates team building
- It focuses attention on project objectives
- It forces detailed planning
- It facilitates the allocation of responsibility for individual packets of work
- It graphically illustrates project scope
- It may be re-useable for similar projects

4.3 Principal Uses of the WBS

The WBS is a necessary input to all of the following:-

- Planning and budgeting
- Scope Definition
- Resource Allocation
- Estimating
- Scheduling
- Controlling
- Configuration management
- Risk Identification

4.4 Scope Baseline

The Project Scope Statement and its associated WBS and dictionary represent the project scope baseline against which any future deviations are measured.

4.5 Other Breakdown structures

There are further kinds of breakdown structures you need to be aware of.

1. **Product Breakdown Structures**—also referred to as a Bill of Materials

2. **Cost Breakdown Structures**—Breaks down the project costs in any desired fashion.

3. **Organisational Breakdown Structures**—Basically a hierarchical organisation chart. Often called a Resource Breakdown Structure

4. **Risk Breakdown Structure**.- A hierarchical depiction of project risks

5 Verify Scope

This is the performance of **acceptance tests** to verify that the finished products are compliant with the client/contractual requirements and scope as defined by the WBS. It is the assurance that all of the project deliverables have actually been achieved. The product of each work package will have an acceptance test to determine whether or not the work has been completed. **Acceptance tests** for final products are generally performed in conjunction with the customer.

6 Control Scope

The principal tool for controlling scope is the Integrated Change Control Process described in the previous chapter. Scope is also controlled by regular performance reporting and reviewing.

6.1 Performance Reports (Work Performance Data)

Performance/progress reports are a means of determining whether the project is on target, that is, to compare actual performance to the project plan with respect to time, cost, quality and scope. Their primary purpose is to identify problems and issues so that corrective action can be taken and to provide an audit trail and project history.

6.2 Some Tools & Techniques for Performance Reporting

- Performance Reviews
- Variance analysis
- Trend analysis
- Earned value analysis
- Exception reports
- Gantt charts
- Milestone charts
- Cost reports e.g. cumulative cost curves

Most organisations will have standard formats and schedules for reporting progress.

6.3 Project Reviews

Reviews fall into two main categories:-

a) Ongoing reviews carried out during the life of the project.
b) Post project reviews (often called lessons learned reviews)

6.4 Ongoing Reviews

Ongoing reviews can be triggered by the following:-

- Major milestones e.g. Phase reviews
- Critical problems
- External request/audit

Typical objectives of an ongoing review are:-

- To examine project status with regard to time cost and quality
- To identify problems and corrective actions
- To clarify and confirm project objectives
- To provide information and reassurance to stakeholders
- To fulfil Quality and Audit requirements

Potential outcomes of an ongoing review include the following:

- Identification of significant risks to the project which require attention
- Significant changes in the project's objectives or scope
- Decision to terminate or change the scope of the project.
- Lessons learned

6.5 Final or Post-Project Review/Evaluation

This is conducted after all project deliverables have been accepted and all other project tasks have been completed. The primary purpose is to identify **lessons learned** so that they can be shared with other project teams. Lessons learned include things done well as well as things done less than well. It includes documenting why variations from the plan took place and why particular protective actions were taken. It is important that the review takes place immediately upon project completion before the project team breaks up and whilst events are fresh in the mind. As previously stated it should be chaired by an independent person. It should cover the following:-

- History of the project
- Performance of the project organisation
- Accuracy of project planning and estimating reasons behind variances between plan and actual
- Suitability of monitoring and control systems
- Suitability of the overall project strategy

It does not consider benefits realisation. This is the subject of the future Post Implementation Review and is the responsibility of the sponsor.

6.6 Potential problems with Post Project Reviews

Some of the potential problems and dangers that can occur with reviews are:-

- There is a danger that management may misuse evaluations to identify and punish poor performers.
- Some people may misuse evaluations to support their own political agendas.
- Project managers and teams and will often resist evaluation because they have things to hide and fear criticism.
- Evaluation can interfere with the project because of the effort required to prepare and conduct it.
- The project team may have disbanded

6.7 Causes of Project Failure

Many project failures can be traced back to poor scope planning and control. The accumulation of many, small, and unplanned changes is known as **scope creep.** The following list is far from comprehensive but shows many other causes of project failure.

- Poor top management commitment
- Poor or no planning
- Corporate goals not understood by junior management
- Over ambitious plans with too little time and resource
- Unqualified resource
- Poor estimating
- Insufficient real data for proper planning
- Plans imposed on the project team from above
- Objectives not clearly understood
- Not enough time allowed for planning
- Lack of control of resources by project manager
- Weak project management
- No delineation of responsibilities
- Poor set up

6.8 Risk/Complexity Trade-off

Risk and uncertainty are covered in detail in Chapter 9. Within the area of Scope Management there is one important consideration to be aware of.

As complexity on a project increases, the probability of missing something when defining the scope of the work is likely to increase. Thus as scope complexity increases, so does risk.

Scope Management Practise Questions

1. Which of the following best describes the primary objective of a project review?

a. To help plan the next project
b. To review the operation of the delivered project
c. To capture all the learnings of the project
d. To tie up all the contractual loose ends

2. Which statement about customer expectations is *not* true?

a. The product or service should be usable as intended.
b. Contractual provisions, including schedule and performance standards, should be met.
c. Changes should be made immediately, and all customer wants should be satisfied without bureaucratic hassle.
d. The seller should assume the responsibility of understanding customer needs and wants and addressing them effectively.

3. The WBS is an input to scope change control because it—

a. Provides information on project objectives
b. Defines the project's scope baseline
c. Defines all project baselines
d. Provides information on scope performance

4. The document that describes the objectives, work content, deliverables, and end product of a project is the—

a. Project charter
b. Product description
c. Project Scope statement
d. WBS

5. Which of the following is not true of the Functional Specification?

a. It defines what the product does
b. It defines how the functionality will be produced
c. It is written in non technical language
d. It specifies performance and quality parameters

6. Maintenance is crucially important to projects but should—

a. Be included as an activity to be performed during the closeout phase
b. Have a separate phase in the life cycle
c. Not be viewed as part of the project life cycle.
d. Always be viewed as a separate project

7. As a *minimum* when should senior management perform periodic project reviews:

a. Major milestone points
b. Phase end
c. Whenever actual performance deviates from plan
d. Quarterly

8. From a top management perspective, the progress of the project is measured in completion of blocks of work over time. What does the project manager plan to use as the basis for the budget, schedule, resource allocation, and scope definition in reporting progress?

a. Project Plan
b. Project charter
c. Work breakdown structure
d. Risk management plan

9. Configuration management is:

a. A means of monitoring and controlling emerging product scope against the scope baseline.
b. The creation of the work breakdown structure.
c. The set of procedures developed to assure that project design criteria are met
d. A mechanism to track budget and schedule variances.

10. A change control system must include all the following except?

a. The paperwork
b. The tracking system
c. Verbal approvals
d. Approval levels

11. Which of the following is not a benefit of the WBS?

a. It calculates when work should take place
b. It focuses attention on project objectives
c. It forces detailed planning
d. It facilitates the allocation of responsibility for individual packets of work

12. Inputs used during scope definition include all of the following except:

a. Stakeholder requirements
b. Project charter
c. Detailed budget
d. Organisational process assets

13. Which one of the following statements is not true regarding project planning responsibilities?

a. The project manager is responsible for project planning.
b. Everyone involved with the project must plan.
c. The functional line managers dictate to the project team certain schedule and cost information that must be planned for.
d. The project manager is responsible for ensuring that the functional line managers have final approval authority for the project plan.

14. Project close out is a process in which all activities must be completed in a business-like fashion. When closing out a contract, the primary consideration of the seller and the buyer is to determine—

a. The profit made on the effort
b. Who is to be notified that the contract is completed
c. If the seller met the contract's specifications
d. What reports are required to close out the contract

15. The result (output) of scope verification on a project is-

a. Inspection of Deliverables
b. Formal acceptance
c. Processed invoices
d. Paid bills

16. Which one of the following activities is not part of the conceptual phase of the project life cycle?

a. Development of detailed cost estimates
b. Determining existing needs or potential deficiencies of existing systems
c. Determining the initial system interfaces
d. Establishing the project organisation

17. All the following information is included in the Project Charter except-

a. Detailed project schedule
b. Responsibilities of the project manager
c. Project manager's relationships with various functional managers
d. Project justification and background

18. All the following statements about a work breakdown structure are true except:

A WBS—

a. Provides a framework for organising and ordering the activities that make up a project
b. Breaks a project down into successively greater detail by level
c. Is a planning tool
d. It specifies how long activities should take and when they should be completed.

19.   A project ends when-

I   The objectives are met
II The objectives will not or cannot be met and the project is terminated
III The contract expires
IV The customer says so

a.   I
b.   III
c.   I and II
d.   II and IV

20. Which of the following statements about the scope statement is true?

a.   Does not include project objectives such as cost, schedule, or quality measures
b.   Includes a description of project assumptions and constraints
c.   Provides a documented basis for preparing the PERT/CPM network
d.   Describes how the WBS will be structured

21. The project charter should be issued by—

a.   The project manager
b.   The head of the performing organization
c.   A manager external to the project
d.   The project sponsor

22. What is the ultimate test of project success?

a.   Meeting Time, Cost & Quality goals
b.   Meeting the customer needs
c.   Exceeding customer expectations
d.   Making a profit

23. Completion of project scope activities is measured against the—

a.   Requirements
b.   Project plan
c.   Scope management plan
d.   WBS

24. Which of the following is not a benefit of Scope Definition?

a.   It facilitates estimating
b.   It provides a baseline
c.   It assigns task responsibility
d.   It shows whether all project deliverables have been achieved

25. A project is not formally approved until completion of

a. A Project Charter
b. Project budget
c. Make-or-buy analysis
d. A project brief

26. Which of the following is not a tool or technique for gathering user requirements?

a. Questionnaires
b. Stakeholder analysis
c. Building prototypes
d. Interviews

27. The greatest degree of uncertainty is encountered during which phase of the project life cycle?

a. Concept
b. Planning
c. Implementation
d. Closeout

28. Scope verification—

a. Improves cost and schedule accuracy, particularly on projects using innovative techniques or technology
b. Is the last activity performed on a project before handoff to the customer
c. Documents the characteristics of the product or service that the project was undertaken to create
d. Differs from quality control in that scope verification is concerned with the acceptance—not the correctness—of the work results

29. Written change orders should be required on—

a. All projects, large and small
b. Large projects
c. Projects with a formal configuration management system in place
d. Projects for which the cost of a change control system can be justified

30. Two fundamental objectives of project control are to—

a. Plan activities to achieve results and manage organizational assets
b. Eliminate unexpected technical problems and identify technical difficulties that require more resources
c. Ensure that resources are available when needed and avoid unplanned increases in the scope of work
d. Have the required material, personnel, and equipment available when needed and ensure that budgeting is adequate

31. The project plan is important in change control because it—

a. Provides the baseline against which changes are managed
b. Provides information on project performance
c. Alerts the project team to issues that may cause problems in the future
d. Is expected to change throughout the project

32. Which of the flowing is not true of Post Project Reviews?

a. Produce recommendations for future projects
b. Identify the causes of plan deviations
c. Are not chaired by the Project Manager or Sponsor
d. Measure project outcome against the business case

33. Which of the following tools is used in scope change control?

a. Variance Analysis
b. Change requests
c. Corrective action
d. The scope statement

34. All the following are inputs to project initiation except the—

a. Product or service description
b. Organization's strategic plan
c. Project selection criteria
d. Project charter

35. In all projects, needs must be tempered by schedule, cost, and resource constraints. Project success depends primarily on—

a. The quality of the schedule and cost control analysis
b. Customer satisfaction
c. Customer compromise in defining its needs
d. Exceeding customer requirements through gold-plating

36. A WBS is a product-oriented "family tree" of project components. Each item in the WBS is generally assigned a unique identifier; these identifiers are known collectively as—

a. The chart of accounts
b. The code of accounts
c. Work package control numbers
d. WBS ID numbers

PRACTICE QUESTION ANSWERS

		Page	**Paragraph**	
1	C	46	6.5	
2	C	45	6	All changes must be evaluated before agreeing to implement them
3	B	44	4.4	The WBS is the foundation upon which the project is built
4	C	42	3	
5	B	42	2.3	The Functional Spec is about "what" not "how"
6	C	12	1.6	Maintenance normally commences after project completion.
7	B	45	6.4	
8	C	44	4.3	
9	A	29	6.5	The configuration must be maintained as changes are made to product scope.
10	C	28	6.3	Just as change requests must be in writing so must approvals
11	A	44	4.2	The WBS what work is required. The Schedule says when it takes place.
12	C	42	3	Scope definition is about what work is required. Costing comes later.
13	D	25	3.1	Final approval rests with the project Sponsor
14	C	44	5	
15	B	44	5	
16	A	13	1.6	
17	A	22	2	
18	D	44	4.3	The WBS should specify how long work should take but when it should be done
19	C	30	7	
20	B	28	6.3	A change in configuration may dictate a change in the schedule but that will not be measured by the configuration control system
21	D	22	2	
22	B	16	1.11	At the end of the day unless customer needs are met all other success criteria are irrelevant.
23	D	44	5	
24	C	42	3	After Scope has been defined by the WBS we can then assign responsibilities
25	A	22	2	
26	B	161	2.3	Although Stakeholders should be interviewed to obtain their requirements this is not stakeholder analysis
27	A	13	1.6	At the start of the project everything is in the future
28	D	44	5	Scope verification involves acceptance testing. It does not guarantee quality
29	A	28	6.3	Formal change control should apply to all projects.
30	C	27	5	Project control will not manage organisational assets, eliminate technical problems or ensure an adequate budget
31	A	28	5	
32	D	46	6.5	
33	A	45	6.2	Only a) is a tool
34	D	13	1.6	The project charter is a product of project initiation
35	B	16	1.11	
36	B	43	4.1	

Chapter 4

Project Time Management

1 Project Time Management Processes

Project Time Management consists of all those processes necessary to ensure that the project is completed on time. The processes are listed below.

1. **Define Activities**

2. **Sequence Activities**

3. **Estimate Activity Resource**

4. **Estimate Activity Duration**

5. **Develop Schedule**

6. **Control Schedule**

These processes do not take place as a series of sequential processes. They react with each other, and with processes in other knowledge areas, and are highly iterative.

The following text will cover the above processes in a sequence more geared towards understanding.

2 Define Activities

2.1 Decomposition

The work of activity definition has mostly been carried out by the creation of the WBS. Each work package is a defined activity. If it is felt necessary, the work package may be decomposed further by the person or team carrying out the work. Whatever the level of decomposition it is the lowest level of the WBS that will be scheduled and each activity will still have a deliverable. (Many authorities do not distinguish between work packages and activities)

2.2 Rolling Wave Planning

Rolling wave planning is the concept by which tasks and activities in the near future are subject to detailed planning whilst tasks further out, or in future phases, are planned in progressively less detail. Note that this process progressively elaborates the project scope but it does not change it.

3 Activity Sequencing & Schedule Development

3.1 Overview of PERT, CPM and PDM

PERT- Program Evaluation and Review Technique

- Has three time estimates per activity: pessimistic (p), most likely (m), and optimistic (o)
- Most likely estimate calculated by formulae $(p + 4m + o)/6$
- Activity on line
- All relationships Finish to Start

CPM - Critical Path Method

- One time estimate per activity
- Activity on line
- All relationships Finish to Start

PDM - Precedence Diagram Method

- Activity-on-node
- Represents an improvement to PERT and CPM by adding other relationships to activities i.e.
  - Start-to-Start
  - Start-to-Finish
  - Finish-to-Finish

Note: There is a further technique called **CDM (Conditional Diagramming Method)** that allows for such things as loops and conditional branches which none of the above techniques support. It is sufficient that you know of its existence. It will not be dealt with further here.

3.2 Activity on Line Networks

Shown below is a simple illustration of an Activity-on-line network for cooking a meal.

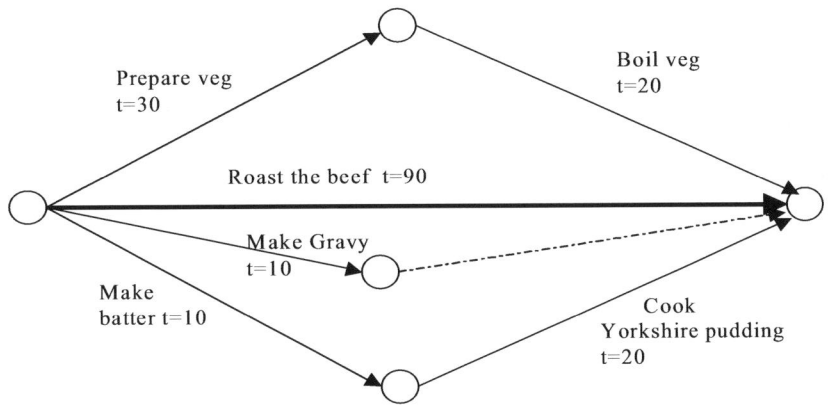

In Activity-on-line (or arrow) the nodes represent events that consume no time and represent the start and end of individual activities. Dummy activities are utilised in activity on arrow networks and their purpose is to show multiple relationships or dependencies among project activities. Dummy activities (dotted lines) consume no time or resources; they are present only to show that a dependency exists between two activities. The Activity-on-Line method can only support Finish to Start relationships.

3.3 Activity on Node Networks

The activity on node method is associated with the Precedence Diagram Method. The activity on line method can only cope with finish-to-start activities. To handle more complex precedence relationship we must use activity on node. Activity on node networks can also incorporate lag, which is defined as waiting time between activities in a network; for example, we order something and must wait for it to arrive or we paint something and must wait for it to dry. Slack is the same as Float but Lag is something completely different. Slack is the amount of time that a particular activity can be delayed without delaying the project.

As you can see below, activity-on-node networks have no need of dummy activities. In the figure above we need a dummy activity to differentiate between the ends of Roast Beef and Make Gravy. In the figure below a dummy activity is not necessary.

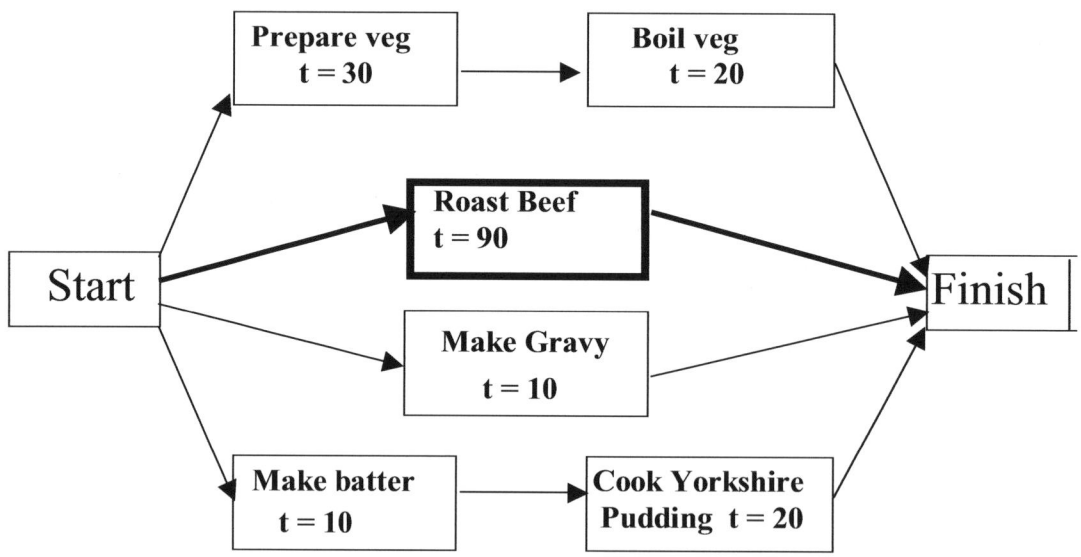

3.4 The Critical Path

The critical path is the longest path through the network. Thus, it is also the shortest amount of time in which the project can be completed. If any activity on the critical path runs over time then so does the whole plan. Adding the times along the critical path gives the expected project duration. The critical path is identified by adding the times along all possible paths. The longest path is the critical path. If two or more paths have the same length then there are multiple critical paths. The critical path always has least slack (float)

3.5 Activity Sequencing

A network is built up by a process known as **Activity sequencing**, which concerns the order in which tasks are performed and which tasks can be performed in parallel. Activity sequencing makes use of the following three types of dependencies.

Mandatory
Mandatory dependencies are often called "hard logic". They involve physical restrictions, which cannot be avoided. e.g. you have to dig the foundations before you pour the concrete.

Discretionary dependencies
 Discretionary dependencies involve sequencing that is done because it is the customary or preferred method but could be done another way, or it may be preferred or mandated by a customer or other important stakeholder. However it is not a physical constraint.

External dependencies
External dependencies exist where is a relationship between project activities and events outside the boundaries of the project.

3.6 Precedence Relationships with Leads and Lags

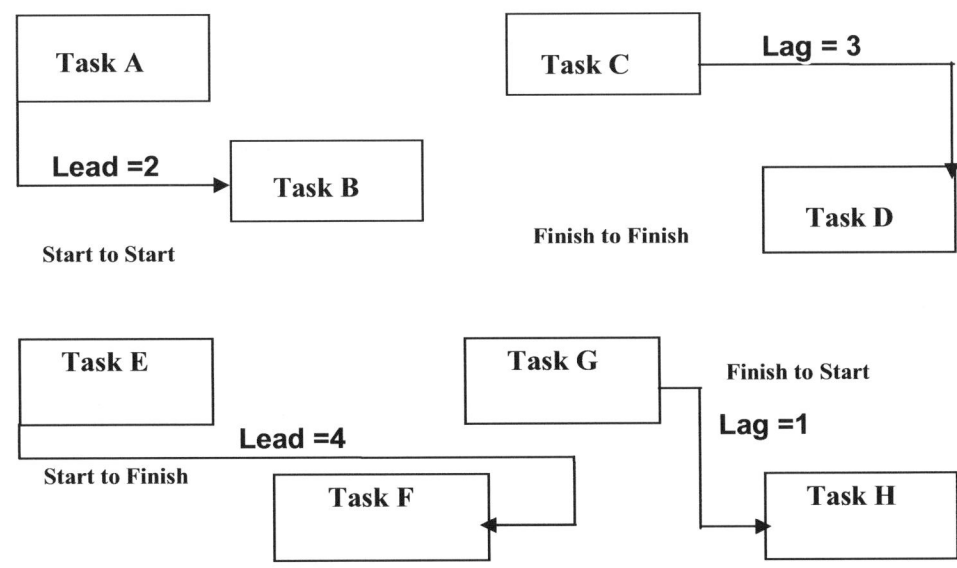

Start to Start
> B can start 2 days after A starts

- **Finish to Finish**
  > D can not finish until 3 days after C finishes

- **Start to Finish**
  F cannot finish until at least 4 days after E starts

- **Finish to Start**
  There is at least 1 day between G finishing and H starting.

- **Leads and lags**
   Leads originate from start times and lags from finish times.

3.7 Float

Activities that are *not* on the Critical Path exhibit Float (or Slack). There are two kinds of Float to consider.

 Total Float is the amount of time that an activity can be delayed without affecting project duration.

Free Float is the amount of time that can be slipped without delaying any immediately following activities.

There are formulae for calculating Total Float and Free Float for both Arrow and Precedence networks. However, as you will find in the examples to follow, you will find it easier to deduce these values from the network rather than memorising and applying the formulae.

3.8 Early Start/Finish & Late Start/Finish

 Early start date and Early finish date denote where the activity starts as soon as possible. *Late start date and Late finish date* denote where the activity has been delayed as long as possible. They are calculated using a *Forward pass and Backward pass* respectively. This will be illustrated in the examples to follow.

3.9 Network Analysis Examples

a) **Activity on Arrow**

Activity	Duration	Dependency
A	10	-
B	5	A
C	20	A
D	5	B
E	5	D
F	5	C
G	10	C&D

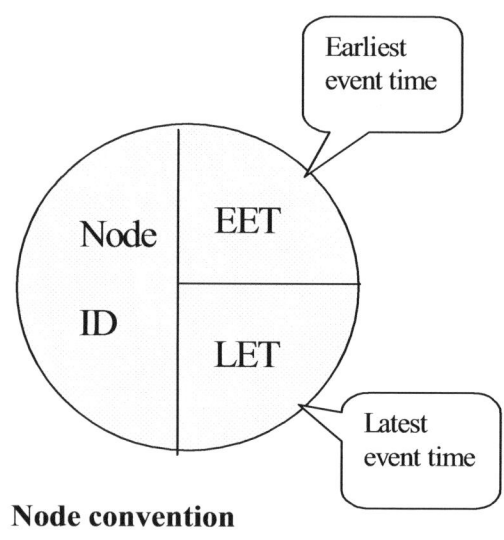

Node convention

Step 1- Construct the network and enter the durations

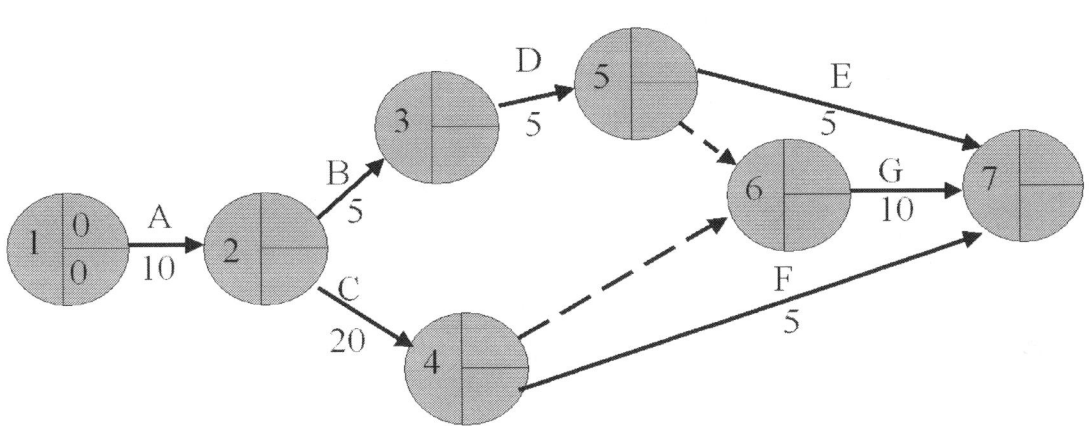

The dotted lines represent dummy activities. They represent multiple dependencies. No two activities are allowed to share the same pair of nodes. Hence the need for dummies. When calculating the network dummies can be treated just like activities except they have zero duration.

Step 2- Carry out the forward pass

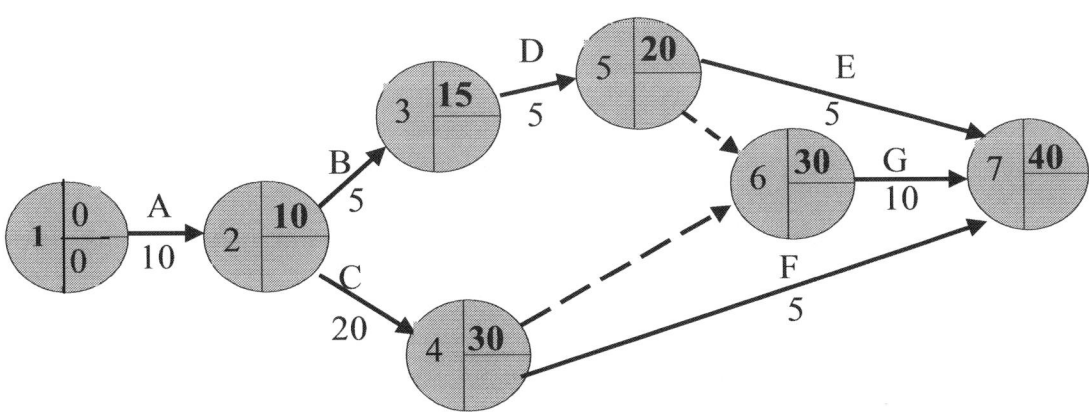

e.g for activity A, 0 + 10 = 10, for activity B 10+5 = 15 etc
Where there are 2 input arrows then we take the largest total i.e. the latest finisher.
Thus for activity G there are 2 inputs. From D we have 20 + 0 (the dummy link is zero). From C we have 30+0. Therefore we select 30, the latest finish.

Step 3-Carry out the backward pass

We reverse the procedure for the backward pass. Thus for activity G 40-10 = 30.
Where 2 backward arrows enter a node we now take the lowest total. Thus for node 2 we have 25 – 5 = 20 from activity B, and 30 –20 = 10 from activity C. Therefore we take 10 which is the earliest.

The critical path follows the nodes where early and late times are the same i.e. A,C,G

Floats can be obtained by inspection or using the following formulae:-

Total float = latest time of finish event - earliest time of start event – duration
Free float = earliest time of finish event – earliest time of start event – duration

b) Activity on Node example

Draw and completely analyse an activity-on-node network for the following project, assuming the project is to be completed in minimum time.

Activity	Duration	Dependency
A	10	NONE
B	15	A
C	5	A
D	8	A
E	2	D
F	10	B,C,E

Step 1- Construct the network and enter the durations

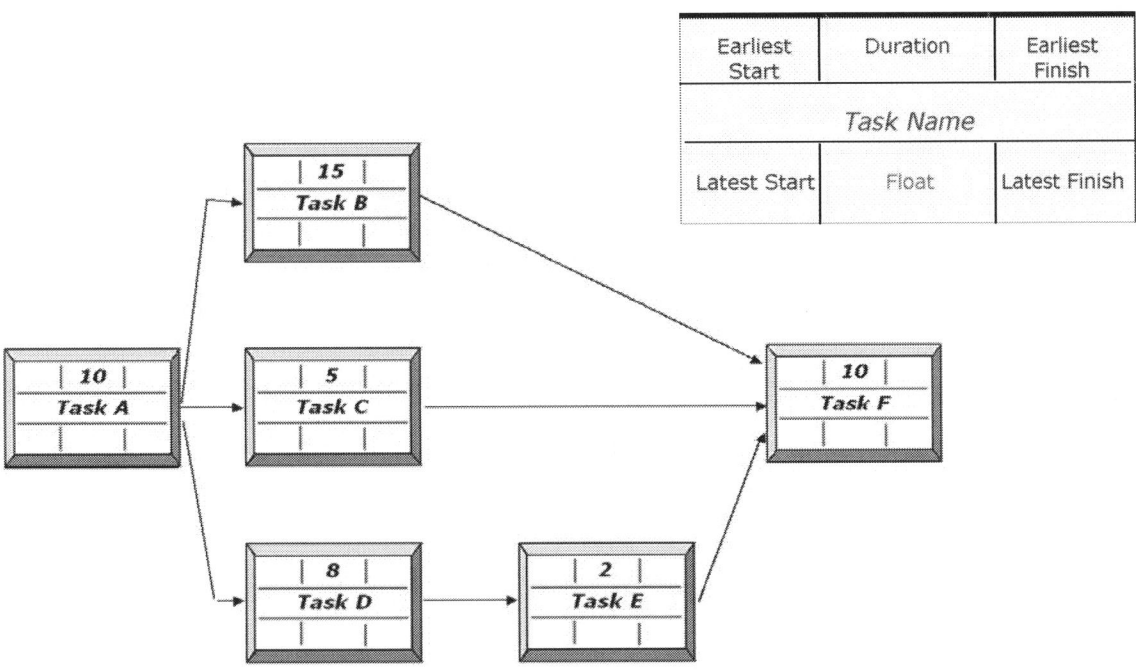

Earliest Start	Duration	Earliest Finish
	Task Name	
Latest Start	Float	Latest Finish

Step 2- Carry out the forward pass

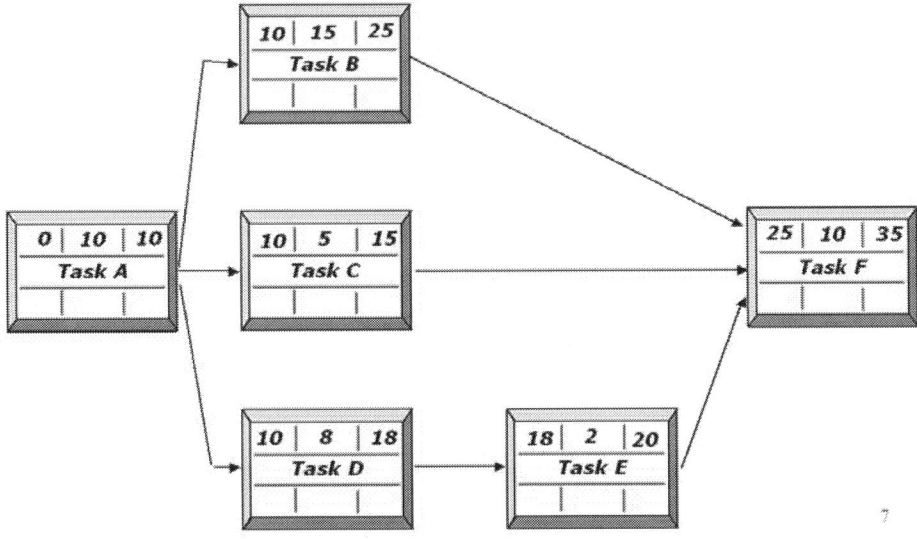

Thus for activity A   0 + 10 = 10. This 10 is carried forward to all the successor activities and so on. Where there are multiple arrows we take the latest (the largest) as before. Thus for activity F we take the largest of 25 (from B), 15(from C) and 20(from E)

Where there are multiple backward arrows e.g. into activity A then as before, we take the smallest which in this case is the 10 from B

Step 3- Carry out the backward pass

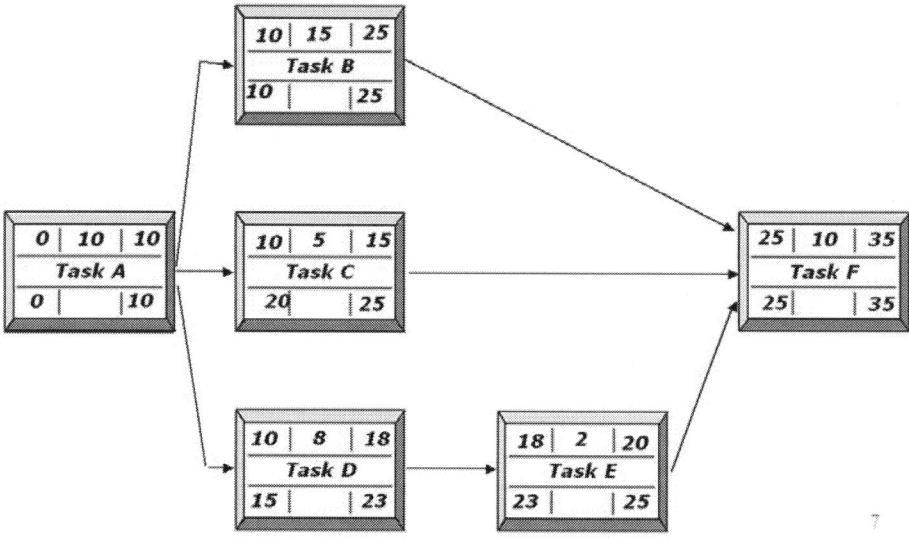

Thus for activity F 35(the finish time) – 10 (duration) = 25 (the start time)
This 25 becomes the latest finish date for B, C and E

Step 4 Calculate Total Float by subtracting the early dates from the late dates.

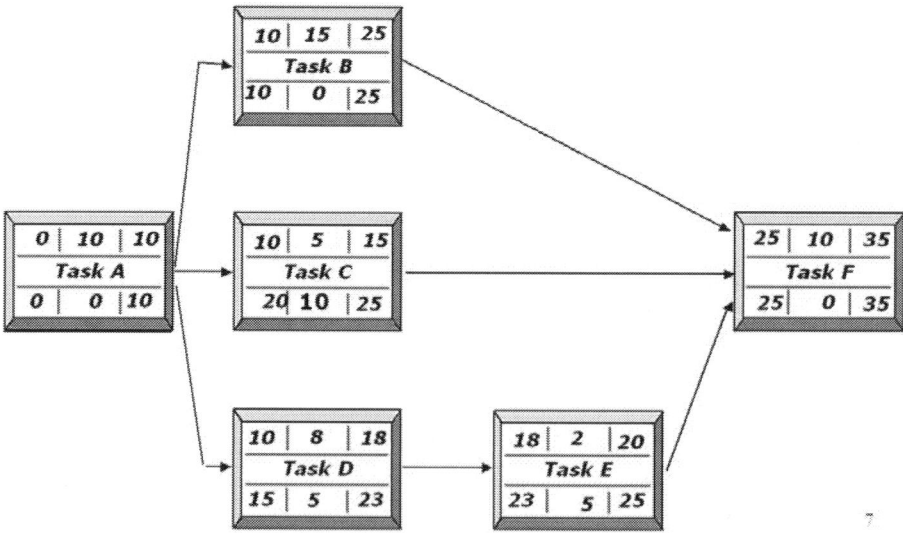

The critical path is the path with least total float, which in this case is zero. A,B,F
Note that in the case of a series of activities such as D and E above the total is not available to all of them. Because of this it is sometimes called shared float.

Free Float by inspection

The example below shows how we can determine free float by inspection rather than have to memorise a formulae

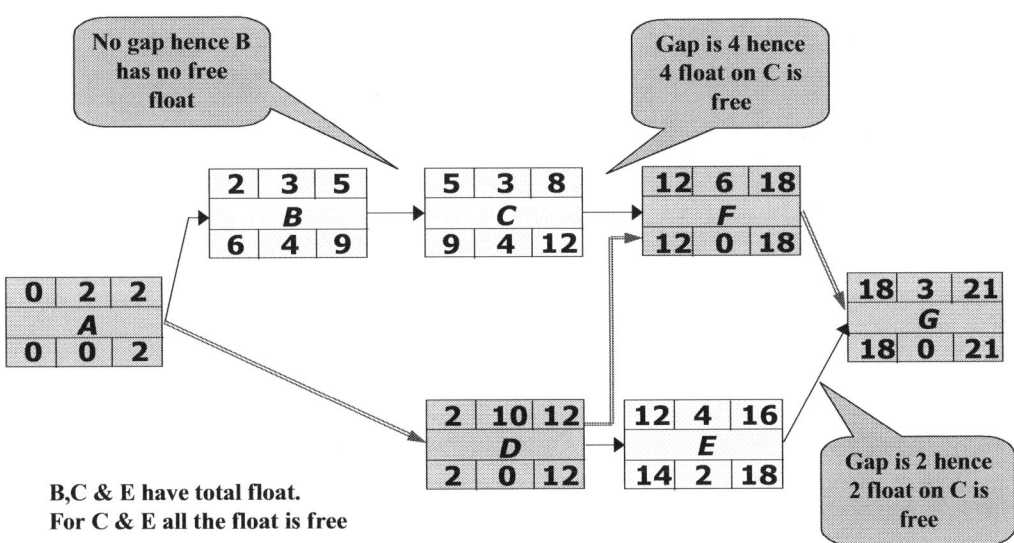

B,C & E have total float.
For C & E all the float is free

3.10 Crashing and Fast Tracking

When projects fall behind schedule there are two techniques, which can be used in an attempt to get back on time. They are **crashing** and **fast tracking**

Crashing involves adding more resources to activities that are on the critical path in order to reduce the elapsed time of those activities. Here are some important guidelines:

1) Focus on activities on the critical path

2) Choose activities that are indeed "crashable" (adding resources to some late tasks may only make them even later)

3) Focus first on the activities in which the cost of crashing is lowest

Crashing the network invariably increases project costs

Fast tracking involves doing more activities in parallel; that is trying to create more parallel paths. Both Fast Tracking and Crashing require more concentrated resources. This approach usually increases risk.

3.11 Resource Allocation

Resource Smoothing   It is normally of great benefit if project resources are used in as uniform a way as possible. All tasks on non-critical paths exhibit float. By using this float i.e. adjusting the timing of tasks, the planner can arrange a schedule of work that attempts to level out the peaks and valleys in the resource plan. Resource smoothing attempts to resolve resource overloads by utilising Float.

Consider this example.

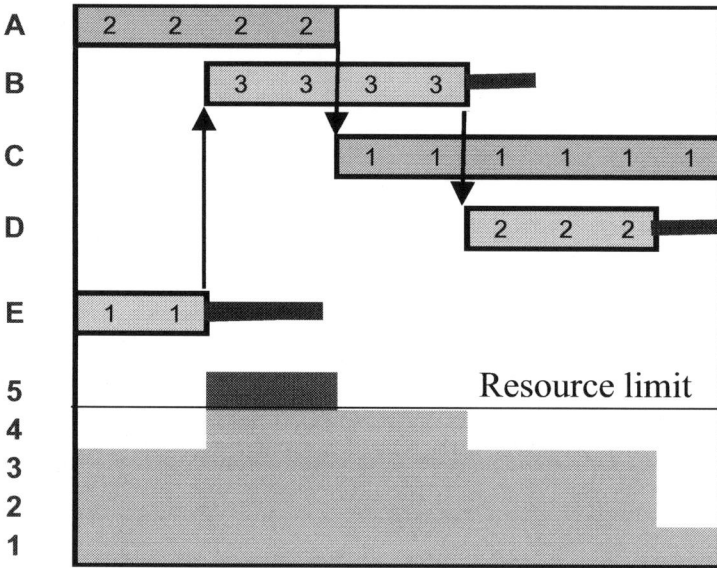

Applying **Resource Smoothing** and utilising the **float** on activity B and D we arrive at the position below. This is a **Time constrained schedule**. Here the network schedule is allowed to change but the end date is retained.

Resource Smoothing

> **Time constrained schedule**
>
> In this case the network schedule is fixed and the program will allocate the required resource.

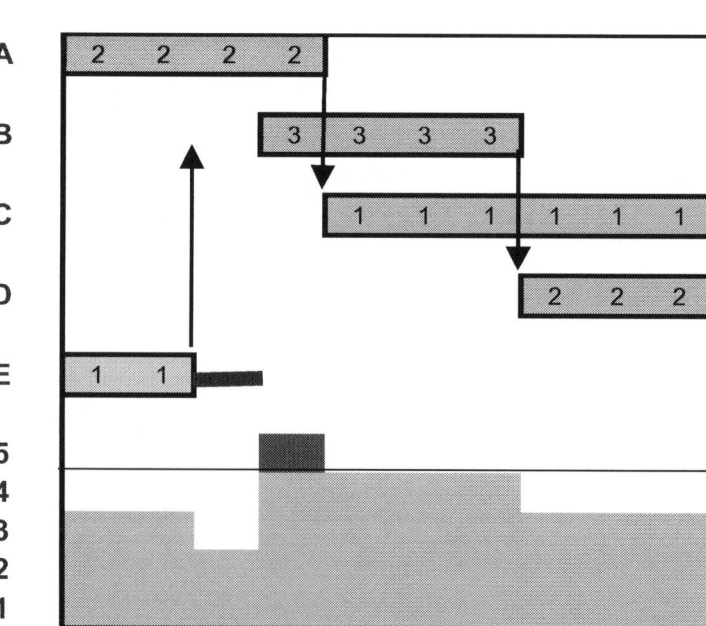

Resource Levelling

In order to fully address the resource overload, in this example we must delay B and hence D thus extending the project. This process of **Resource Levelling** is resource constrained and the outcome is shown below.

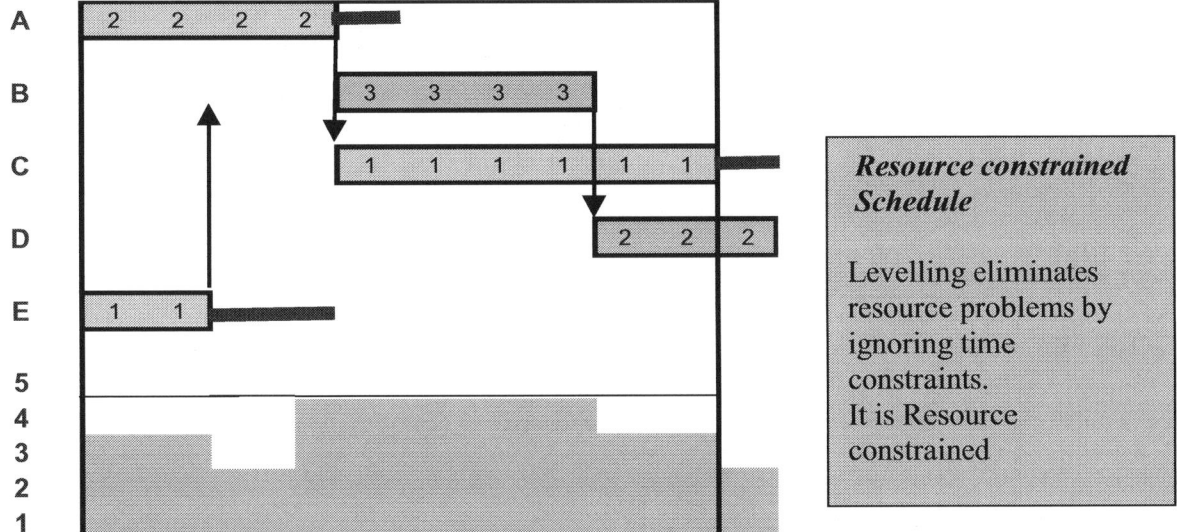

Resource constrained Schedule

Levelling eliminates resource problems by ignoring time constraints.
It is Resource constrained

4 Activity Estimating

Although **Resource** and **Duration** estimating are treated by PMI as two separate processes in practice they are interdependent and should be considered together.

Common tools are:

4.1 Analogous Estimating:

This is where we use information based on similar projects done in the past. It is a *top-down* estimating method and is a form of *expert judgement*.

4.2 Published Estimating Data

In many industries there is published data which provides standardised time and resource estimates for known tasks e.g Construction, Servicing. This is sometimes referred to as the *"Blue Book"*

4.3 Parametric Estimating (See Cost module 2.4)

This is where we use simple mathematical relationships based on standard or historic date. e.g. number of bricks laid per hour to estimate how long to build a wall.

4.4 Bottom-up Estimating

This involves breaking the work up into more detail and then aggregating the individual detailed estimates.

It is important to recognise that the above tools are not mutually exclusive and are usually applied together.

4.5 Three point estimating (PERT estimating)

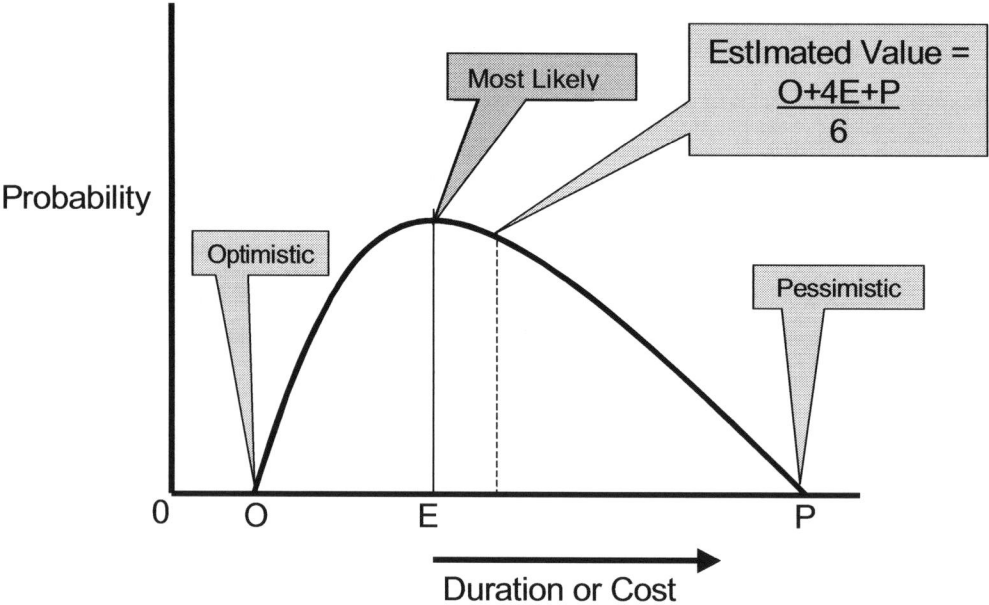

This method recognises the inherent risk in measuring activity durations. It involves making Optimistic, Most Likely and Pessimistic estimates. A simple weighted average can be used to arrive at a single value (PERT formulae) or the 3 estimates can be used in a more sophisticated manner such as Monte Carlo Simulation

4.6 Monte Carlo Simulation

Monte Carlo simulation is a computer based technique, which simulates the project outcomes many times to form a distribution of possible outcomes. It does this by sampling from the above Beta distribution for every activity. It is called Monte Carlo because it relies on the generation of random numbers (e.g. as on a roulette wheel) to simulate real life. It yields a range of possible outcomes (cost and schedule are usually of particular interest) and provides the probability for each outcome. This process gives a project manager much better information for planning a project. The outcome of a Monte Carlo simulation is illustrated above opposite. (see also Risk page 186)

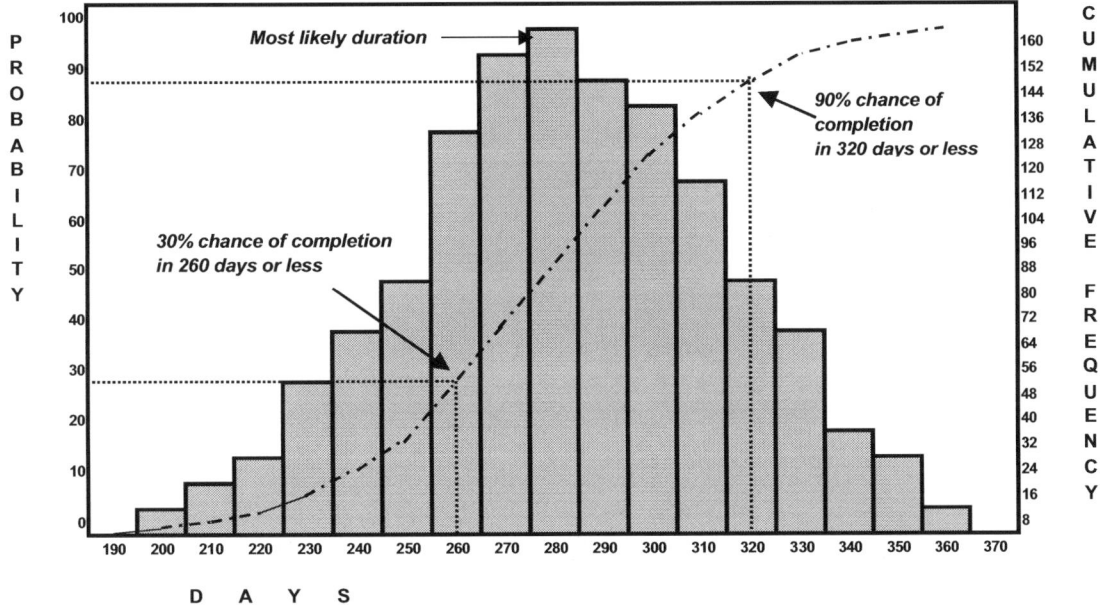

*Note that CPM and PERT will tend to **understate** project durations by comparison to Monte Carlo analysis. This is due to the phenomenon known as **path convergence.** (See page 186)*

4.7 Critical Path Standard Deviation

By using the 3 point estimate we can calculate a very good approximation to the **standard deviation** of each task and calculate the standard deviation of the critical path. We estimate the **standard deviation** if each task using the formulae (P-O)/6. We then take the square of each task to form the Variance. Then add up all the variances along the critical path and take the square root of the total. This is the standard deviation of the critical path. A fuller explanation is given in the Quality chapter, pages 114,115.

4.8 Contingency Reserve

In order to recognise the inherent risk in making estimates it is normal to incorporate additional time and resource within the budget to allow for possible overruns. Such a reserve can be allocated task by task or at higher levels within the WBS.

5 Relative Advantages of Scheduling Tools

5.1 Networks (PERT, CPM, PDM)

Networks provide a visible representation of relationships between project activities and events Networks identify the project duration, the critical path and the relationships between activities.

5.2 Bar chart (Gantt Chart)

- A "pure" Gantt chart is a weak planning tool

(Note so called Gantt charts produced by MS Project etc are in reality networks drawn to look like Gantt charts. The original Gantt chart was simply a bar chart)

- It is effective in reporting progress
- Does not illustrate logical relationships between activities

5.3 Milestone Chart

- Shows only significant/major events on the project
- Useful in communicating overall project status
- Milestones are events that have zero duration

6 Schedule Control

6.1 Types of schedules

1. **Milestone Schedule.** Identifies key events that represent the completion of an activity or group of activities
2. **Summary Schedule.** A bar chart representation that summarises related items of work but does not show individual task details
3. **Detailed schedule**

6.2 Schedule Control Objectives

1. To influence the factors that affect the schedule and make sure changes are beneficial
2. To know when schedule changes have taken place
3. To manage changes when they occur by taking appropriate corrective action.

6.3 Progress Reporting

1. **Performance reviews.** These are meetings held to assess project status and/or progress. They are typically used with one or more of the performance-reporting techniques described below

2. **Variance analysis.** Variance is simply Plan minus Actual. Therefore, if a task was planned to take 3 days and it actually takes 5 days, the schedule variance would be equal to minus 2 days. (Do not confuse this Variance with Statistical Variance which equals the square of the standard deviation, see Quality page 115)

   Variance analysis involves comparing actual project results to planned or expected results. Cost and schedule variances are the most frequently analysed, but variances from plan in the areas of scope, resource, quality, and risk are often of equal or greater importance.

3. **Trend analysis**. Trend analysis involves examining project results over time to determine if performance is improving or deteriorating.

4. **Earned value analysis**. Earned value analysis in its various forms is the most commonly used method of performance measurement. It integrates scope, cost (or resource), and schedule measures to help the project management team assess project performance. It is covered in the Cost Module

6.4 Baselines

Project control is about the *schedule baseline* and any changes that might occur.

- The schedule baseline is the original, approved project schedule and becomes the standard used to measure schedule performance
- The baseline should never be changed without proper review and approval.
- Change requests may occur in numerous ways but any approved change should be documented in writing.
- Changes may either extend or accelerate the schedule.
- Re-baselining can become necessary if the original schedule was so unrealistic that reporting against it is pointless.
- *Changes almost always increase the project cost!*

6.5 Critical Chain Scheduling

Critical Chain is a fairly recent concept that offers a new way to control projects. Its basic premise is that activities have built in contingencies and therefore many activities should finish early.

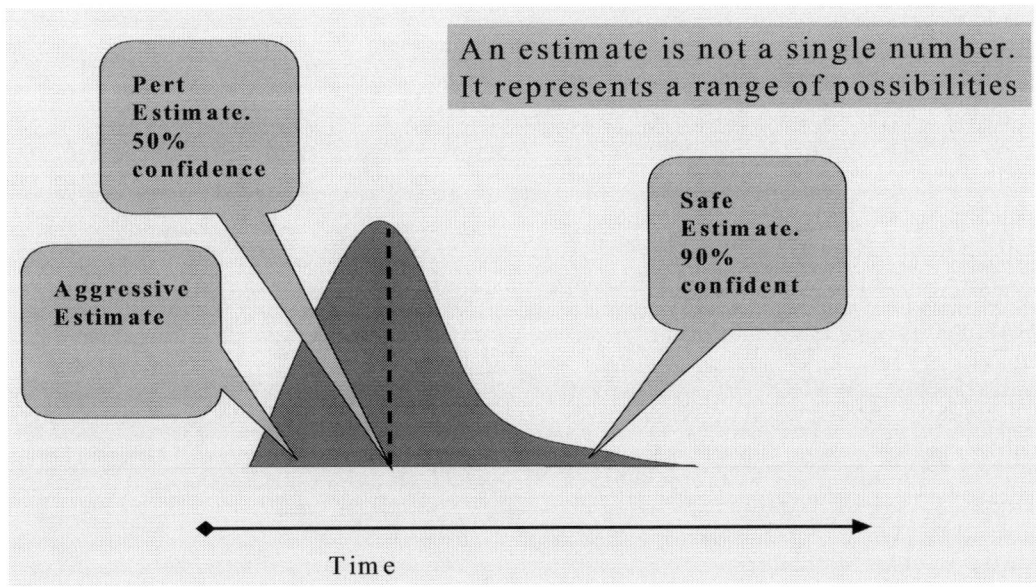

In general, critical activities that finish late invariably delay project completion but when they finish early we often fail to take advantage because subsequent activities are not ready to commence.

The Critical Chain approach is to give every activity an aggressive time scale, recognising that most of them will be late. The total contingencies are accumulated as a **buffer** that is consumed by delayed activities. The emphasis is on managing the buffer and making sure that subsequent activities are ready to start as soon as they are able. The total project buffer would typically be only 50% of the total accumulated contingencies thus, in theory, delivering a shorter project. As well as a total project

buffer there is also a buffer on each non critical path at the point where they reach the critical path. These are known as feeder buffers. This concept is illustrated below

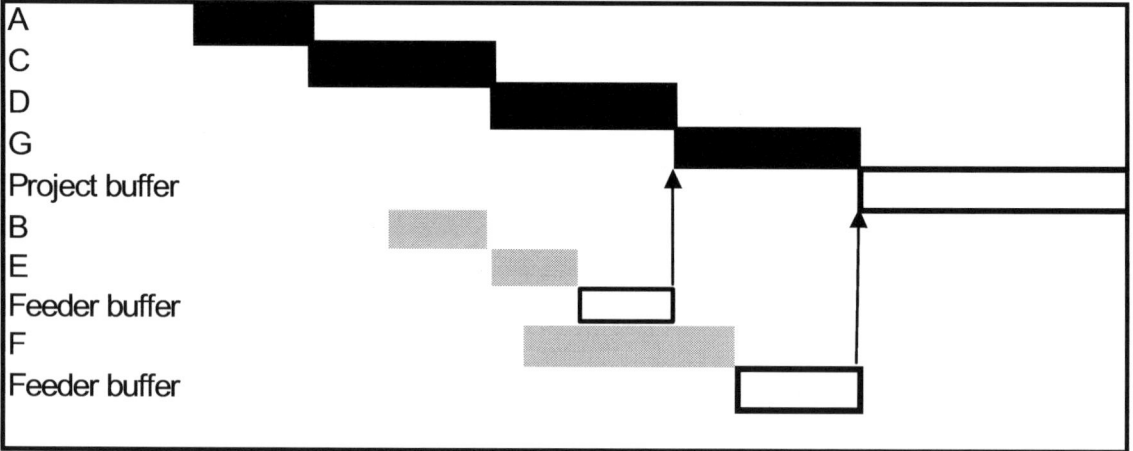

The principal governing the use of Critical Chain are as follows:-

1 Use average estimates for task duration

2 Cut estimates in half

3 Create buffers for critical path and feeder chains

4 Buffer lengths should be half the time removed

5 Create the schedule by working backwards

6 Control the plan by managing the buffers

Applying these principles leads to a project plan that has its planned duration reduced to 75% of the original.

7 Other Concepts

7.1 Heuristics (Rule of Thumb)

Heuristics is a word that simply means guidelines or "rules of thumb" that have been learned through experience or trial and error. *(The expression "rule of thumb" comes from the ancient practice of using the width of the thumb as a rough measure.)* A Heuristic is usually in the form of a simple formula, which has been found to give acceptable results. The PERT estimate for activity duration is a good example. Another example is the PERT formula for standard deviation:

i.e. $\sigma = (p-o)/6$ i.e. (pessimistic –optimistic)/6

7.2 Estimating Accuracy

Duration estimates using PERT are more pessimistic i.e. realistic than the single time estimate used in original CPM calculations. This is because the approach forces people to consider a range of outcomes and thus to some extent counteracts the optimism often found in schedule estimates.

Duration estimates should always include some indication of the range of possible outcomes. e.g 3 point estimating

Estimating, especially for complex projects, is exceedingly difficult and is a major cause of project time and cost overruns.

7.3 Subnets

Repeatable elements of a network (akin to a software subroutine).

Also called fragnets.

Time Management Practice Questions

1. Which one of the following is not a definition of the critical path?

    a) The path with least float
    b) The longest path in the network
    c) The shortest possible planned project duration
    d) The path having zero float

2. In calculating dates in a network diagram, the forward pass results in the calculation of—

    a) The critical path
    b) Float for non-critical activities
    c) The early start and late finish dates
    d) The early start and early finish dates

3. Which one is true? An activity-on-arrow diagram—

    a) Illustrates activities by boxes, and dependencies by arrows
    b) Supports Finish-to-Finish and Start-to-Start relationships
    c) Needs to utilise dummy activities to define some logical relationships
    d) Shows the total float value

4. PERT is an estimating tool that-

    a) Incorporates risk as an element of the estimate
    b) Can only be used for estimating level of effort
    c) Can only be used in the precedence diagram method.
    d) Uses only historical estimates to calculate standard deviations

5. Fast tracking requires greater project control, because it is a practice that increases _____ while shortening project _____ .

    a) Benefit cost ratio, actual cost of work performed
    b) Budgeted cost of work performed, scheduled end date
    c) Risk, duration
    d) Level of effort, late finish date

6. The difference between fast tracking and crashing is best described by which one of the following statements-

a. There is no difference
b. Fast tracking involves dealing with cost constraints; crashing is concerned with   schedule problems
c. Fast tracking attempts to finish a project earlier than schedules; crashing   attempts to complete the project on schedule at no additional cost
d. Fast tracking involves changing the approach to perform activities in parallel; crashing adds resources to project tasks for earlier completion

7.   Schedule control is concerned with-

I) Influencing the factors that create schedule changes to ensure that changes are beneficial
II) Determining that the schedule has changed
III) Managing the actual changes when and as they occur

a) I and II
b) I and Ill
c) II and III
d) I, II, and III

8. PERT is an estimating strategy that is-

a) Optimistic
b) Pessimistic
c) More optimistic than CPM
d) More pessimistic than CPM

9. What is the heuristic formulae for estimating standard deviation of PERT estimates?

a) SD $= (p-o)/6$
b) SD $= (o-p)/6$
c) SD $= (p-o)/4$
d) none of the above

10. If task A has 15 days free float and 25 days total float and the early start date is delayed 30 days what is the effect on the project ?

a) The following task will be delayed 15 days
b) The project is delayed 30 days
c) The project will be delayed 5 days
d) Both a & c

11. Which is true? In Activity-on-Line networks dummy activities .....

a) represent optional dependencies between nodes
b) are those which only require untrained staff
c) do not require the use of human resources
d) are required if otherwise two or more activities would share the same pair of nodes

12.   In the following network which of the following is not true

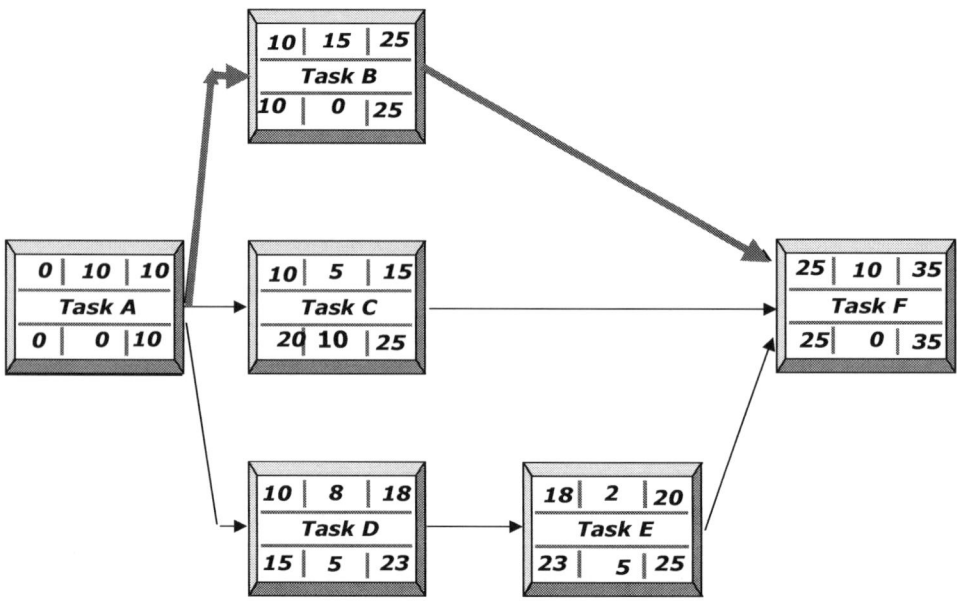

a)   Task C has 5 more days free float than task E
b)   Tasks D & E between them have 10 days total float
c)   Task D has no free float
d)   The critical path is 5 days longer than the next critical path

13. When using Critical Chain Scheduling what is the effect on the original project plan

a)   Reduces duration by 25%
b)   Reduces duration by 50%
c)   Takes away all contingency
d)   No difference

14. Which term describes a change to a logical relationship that delays a successor task?

a) Lag
b) Lead
c) Float
d) Slack

15. The following table shows 3-point estimates for a project critical path measured in days. To the nearest day what is the standard deviation of the critical path?

	Optimistic	Must likely	Pessimistic
Act. A	4	7	10
Act. B	6	13	18
Act. H	4	8	10
Act. F	7	18	25

a) 5 days
b) 4 days
c) 3 days
d) 2 days

16. In any network diagram, slack/float is found when—

a) Early start and late start are not equal
b) Early start and late finish are not equal
c) Late finish plus lag is greater than zero
d) Early start and late finish equal zero

17. If a project's activities have durations that cannot be estimated with a reasonable degree of accuracy, the appropriate method to use is-

a) Critical path method
b) Flow chart methods
c) Program evaluation and review techniques
d) Precedence diagram method

18. The most important document to help a project manager control the project is the

a) Contract specifications
b) Work breakdown structure
c) Project requirements document
d) Risk management plan

19. If staffing levels are constrained to less than the amount required, this will—

a) Require more staff in the long run
b) Push out the end date of the project
c) Reduce total manpower costs for the project
d) Have no effect on the schedule

20.   If the project manager decides to include *subnets or fragnets* in the schedule what would that decision say about the project?

  a)   The project plan requires repetitive feedback loops
  b)   It is too complicated and must be broken down into smaller fragments
  c)   Several identical series of activities are repeated throughout the project.
  d)   Multiple critical paths exist in the project.

21. To assess the implications of crashing a project, a project manager should first compute—

  a)   The cost and time slope for each critical activity that can be expedited
  b)   The cost of additional resources to be added to the project's critical path
  c)   The time that will be saved in the overall schedule when tasks are expedited on the critical path
  d)   Three probabilistic time estimates of PERT for each critical path activity

22. In your project bricklaying can start 1 day after foundations have been poured. This is an example of--

  a)   Start to Start with Lag
  b)   Start to Finish with Lead
  c)   Finish to Start with Lag
  d)   Start to Start with Lead

23. An activity has an early start date of the 10th and a late start date of the 19th. The activity also has a duration of 4 days. There are no non work days. From the information given, what can be concluded about the activity?

  a)   Total float for the activity is 9 days.
  b)   The early finish date of the activity is the end of the day on the 14th.
  c)   The late finish date is the 25th.
  d)   The activity can be completed in 2 days if the resources devoted to it are doubled.

24. Conditional diagramming methods are used—

  a)   To show the four types of dependencies (finish-to-start, finish-to-finish, start-to-start, and start-to-finish)
  b)   To provide additional information to help clarify the network.
  c)   Because standard networking methods do not cater for situations such as loops or conditional branches
  d)   Where things are too complicated for arrow and precedence networks.

25. The basis for measuring and reporting schedule performance is the—

a) Schedule baseline
b) Number of change requests
c) Difference between planned and actual events and activities
d) Technical baseline

26. The tool that provides a basis to identify the work that must be scheduled is the

a) Master schedule
b) Budget
c) WBS
d) Gantt chart

27. Several types of float are found in project networks. Float that is used by a particular activity and does not affect the float in later activities is called—

a) Extra float
b) Free float
c) Total float
d) Expected float

28. Re-baselining may be needed to—

a) Show that the project is not behind schedule
b) Provide realistic data to measure performance
c) Report schedule updates
d) Hide poor performance

29. Which of the following should be a consideration when developing activity time estimates?

a) Resource capabilities
b) Expert judgment
c) Simulation
d) Monte Carlo analysis

30. The major difference between PERT and CPM is that PERT—

a) Uses the distribution's weighted average in computing the schedule
b) Uses the most likely estimate to compute float
c) Focuses on calculating float to determine which activities have the least scheduling flexibility
d) Includes non-sequential activities such as loops or conditional branches as part of the diagram

31. Corrective action in project time management primarily concerns—

a) Analysing reasons behind variances
b) Expediting to ensure that activities remain on schedule
c) Assessing the project management software used
d) Determining the magnitude of any variances

32. Which of the following is the best way of fast tracking a project?

a) Elimination of Float
b) Maximising parallel work
c) Increasing resources
d) Removing contingency

33. A milestone is best described as—

a) A combination of related activities and events
b) An intersection of two or more lines or arrows commonly used for depicting an event or activity
c) An identifiable point in a project that denotes a reporting requirement or completion of an important activity
d) A specific project task that requires resources and time to complete

34. A task has 5 days free float and 10 days total float. Its start is delayed 7 days. What is the effect?

a) The project is delayed by 2 days
b) The project is not delayed
c) The following task slips at least 2 days
d) b + c

35. In project time management, crashing means—

a) Reducing project duration by redefining logical relationships
b) Reducing computer network downtime for schedule risk modelling
c) Applying additional resources to all project activities
d) Applying additional resources to critical path activities by priority

36. All the following are characteristics of a dummy activity *except* that it—

a) Is used primarily in activity-on-arrow networks
b) Has zero duration
c) Requires resources
d) Indicates a precedence relations

PRACTICE QUESTION ANSWERS

		Page	Paragraph	
1	A	58	3.4	The whole project may have float in which case each critical activity will have that same total float
2	D	60	3.8	
3	C	57	3.2	
4	A	68	4.5	b,c,d are false. Only a) is true
5	C	65	3.10	
6	D	65	3.10	
7	D	70	6.2	
8	D	68	4.5	Because the duration distribution of a PERT estimate is usually skewed the PERT estimate is usually higher than the most likely value hence is more pessimistic.
9	A	73	7.1	
10	D			If delay is 30 and FF is 15 then a) is true. If delay is 30 and TF is 25 then c) is true. Hence answer is d).
11	D	61	Step 1	
12	B	64	Step 4	d) and e) share 5 days total float
13	A	71	6.5	
14	A	59	3.6	
15	B	73	7.2	sd = (p-o)/6 A=(10-4)/6 = 1 B=(18-6)/6=2 H=1 F=3: Sums of squares = 1+4+1+9 =15; Nearest answer to square root = 4
16	A	64	Step 4	
17	C	68	4.5	PERT estimating allows you to specify a range of values
18	B	42	4	The whole project is built on the WBS
19	B	67	3.11	This is resource levelling
20	C	73	7.3	
21	A	65	3.10	
22	D	59	3.6	
23	A	60	3.7	A quick way to calculate total float is late start date - early start date
24	C	57	3.1	
25	A	70	6.3	
26	C	56	2.1	
27	B	60	3.7	
28	B	71	6.4	
29	A	67	4	Whatever estimating method is used the results should always reflect the capability of the resources
30	A	68	4.5	
31	B	70	6.2	
32	B	65	3.10	
33	C	70	6.1	
34	D	60	3.7	Total float is more than the delay hence the project will not be delayed. Free float is less than the delay hence the following activity will be delayed
35	D	65	3.10	
36	C	61	Step 1	a), b) and d) are true

Chapter 5

Project Cost Management

1 Project Cost Management Processes

Project Cost Management consists of all those processes necessary to ensure that the project is delivered to budget.

The major processes are:-

1.1 Estimate Costs

Developing as accurately as possible the costs of all the resources need to complete the project

1.2 Determine Budget

Aggregating the above costs for each activity on a timeline to establish a cost baseline

1.3 Control Costs

Influencing and controlling factors that cause changes and variances to the project budget.

Although presented as three separate processes in reality they overlap and interact in a complex fashion.

2 Estimate Costs

In many instances costs are directly related to time so the methods described for estimating times are also appropriate for estimating costs. The following are some tools and techniques for estimating costs.

2.1 Analogous Estimating

Analogous estimating relies on knowledge gained from previous, similar projects. It is a form of top down estimating generally used in the initiation stage of a project. Estimates are generally very approximate.

2.2 Resource Cost Rates

The determination of unit costs such as staff costs /day or bulk material costs/ ton

2.3 Bottom Up Estimating (using the WBS)

Because the WBS identifies project activities that will need resources and also identifies all the work that must scheduled and will require expenditures it is the basis for estimating project costs. Costs are normally controlled at one level above the work package. This level is known as the **Cost Account**. According to PMI the cost account is the lowest level in a project at which organisational responsibilities are assigned and the basic level at which performance is measured.

2.4 Parametric Estimating

Parametric estimating is derived from mathematical relationships. Examples are:-

a) Building costs can be estimated by applying historical costs per square meter based on previous similar buildings
b) Software development costs can be estimated from the forecasted lines of code or by carrying out a function point analysis.

Parametric estimating is also a form of analogous estimating.

2.5 Contingency Allowances

a) **Known unknowns** – Contingency allowances for known work contained within the baseline budget.
b) **Unknown unknowns** – Contingency allowances for unforeseen work outside the baseline budget.

2.6 Accuracy of estimates

Rough order of magnitude (ROM) estimates are approximations without detailed data, often done early in a project. These are often based on analogous methods. Such estimates typically have an accuracy range of +-50 %.Budget estimates are more accurate and are often used to establish initial funding and to gain project approval. The range of accuracy could typically be +-10%. Definitive estimates are used to establish the project cost baseline. They are invariably done bottom up. The accuracy range should be within 5%.

The history and supporting detail behind all estimates should be documented.

3 Determine Budget

Cost budgeting involves aggregating the estimated costs of all work packages over time to establish a total cost baseline for measuring project progress. Consider the following example.

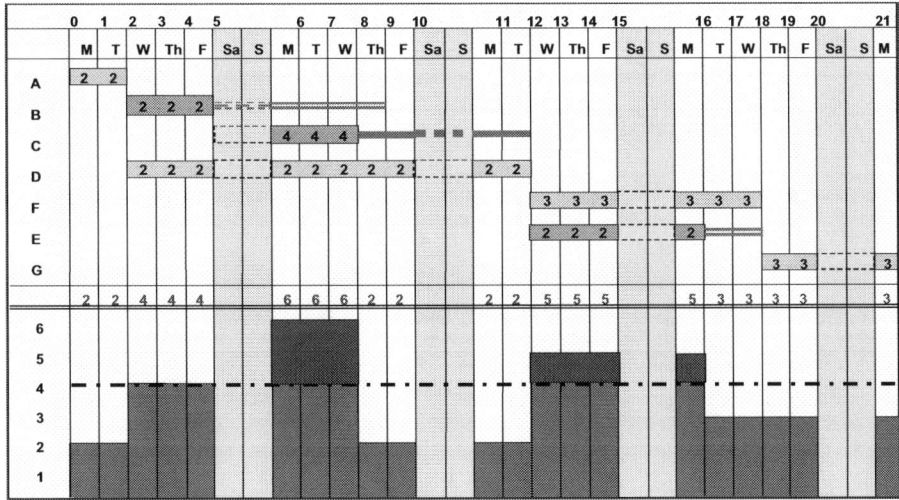

Imagine each resource above cost £500/day. Then we can show the daily costs as follows and then calculate the cumulative cost curve and plot it as shown

Week	1	2	3	4	5	6	7	8	9	10	11	12	13	14	15	16	17	18	19	20	21
Resource	2	2	4	4	4	6	6	6	2	2	2	2	5	5	5	5	3	3	3	3	3
Cost £K	10	10	20	20	20	30	30	30	10	10	10	10	25	25	25	25	15	15	15	15	15
Cum Cost	10	20	40	60	80	110	140	170	180	190	200	210	235	260	285	310	325	340	355	370	385

£K

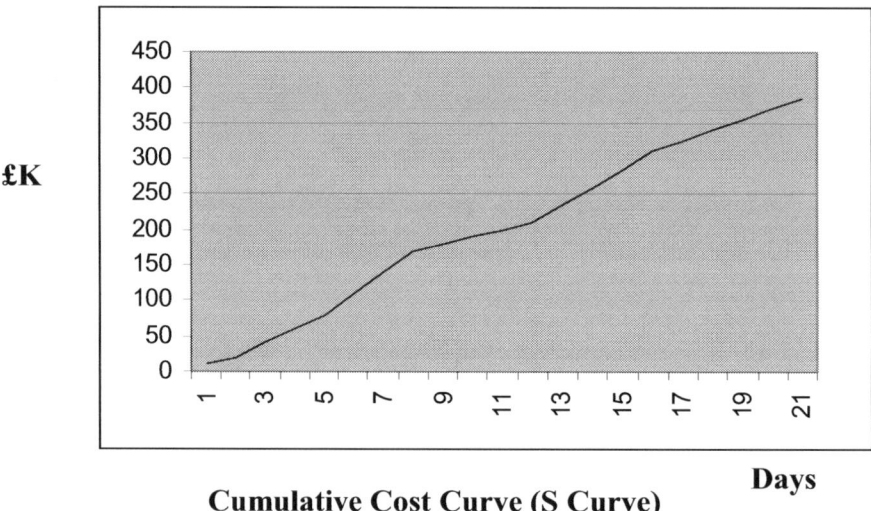

Days

Cumulative Cost Curve (S Curve)

This is the **budget curve** or **cost baseline or PV, the Planned Value**. It represents the planned cost of the planned work. It is the basis of **Earned Value Accounting.** This is the primary tool for **Cost (& Schedule) Control**

3.1 Budget Exercise

From the data below plot the Project S-Curve

Activity	Description	Budget £K	Start time	Duration (weeks)
A	Design hardware	20	0	20
B	Build hardware	40	20	20
C	Procure test facility	10	20	10
D	Test hardware	4	40	5
E	Design software	30	0	30
F	Code software	26	30	20
G	Design tests	5	30	5
H	Test system	15	50	10

Answer at end of chapter.

4 Earned Value Accounting

Earned Value is all about quantifying the value of useful work done rather than what has been spent. In Earned Value terms the value of a completed piece of work is its budgeted value irrespective of what it coat.

4.1 Example

You have just employed a bricklayer to build a wall. The wall in question contains 1,000 bricks which the bricklayer estimates will cost 50p each. He is going to charge you £ 50 per day for the estimated 10 days of work. So the total planned cost of the wall is £1,000.

In Earned Value Management terms this expected cost is the **Planned Value (PV) (This is the cumulative cost curve)**

You have planned to pay for the wall in two instalments of £500. One after 5 days and the other on completion in 10 day's time.

After five days you receive a bill for £ 375. This is the **Actual Cost (AC)**

Your first reaction is "great", he must have got the bricks cheaper than we thought. I've saved £ 125.

You draw the graph below to show how actual expenditure is running below planned expenditure.

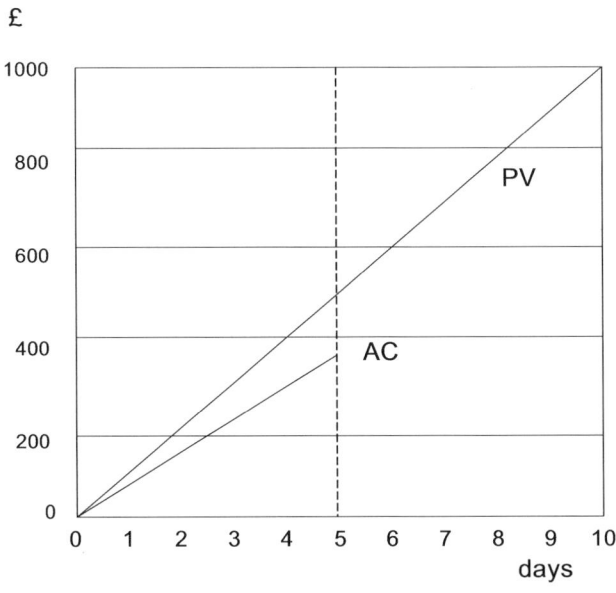

But is this really good news? You call the bricklayer and he tells you he is halfway there. Just to make sure you visit the wall. To your horror you find that only 250 bricks have been laid. Based on the original estimate of £ 1,000 for a wall of 1,000 bricks, the "value" of each brick laid is £ 1.

The value of the work done so far is therefore only £ 250. This is the **Earned Value (EV)**

Let's add this to the graph.

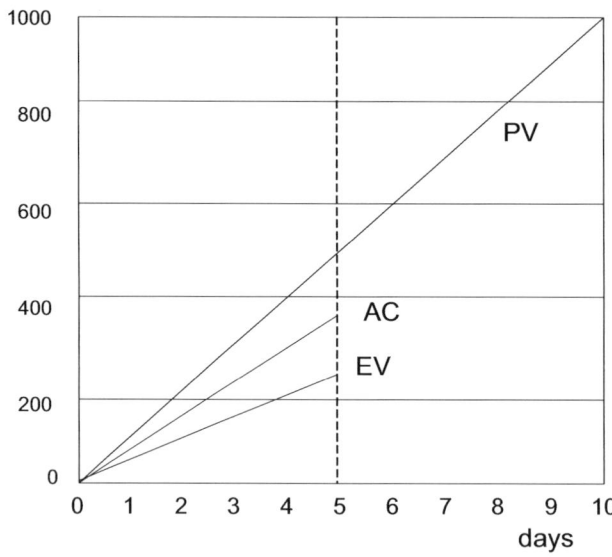

Not only have you paid £375 for what you thought was going to cost £250, but only a quarter of the wall has been finished when it should have been a half.

Let's quantify what's happened.

We can calculate **Schedule Variance (SV)**

SV = Earned Value (EV) – Planned Value (PV)   = 250 - 500 = -250

We can also calculate **Cost Variance (CV)**

CV = Earned Value (EV) - Actual cost (AC)   = 250 - 375 = -125

Both are negative indicating that the project is behind schedule and over budget.

4.2 The Cumulative Cost Curve ("S" Curve)

As previously explained, the project budget can be represented by a Cumulative Cost Curve. This is often called the Budget Curve or, because of its typical shape, the "S" Curve.

The curve shows for any point in time the total planned spend to date. Project progress can be shown by plotting the Actual Costs (AC) to date and the Earned Value (EV) to date. The end of the curve represents the Budget at Completion.

Earned Value is computed for all activities completed or started and equals Planned Value (PV) x %age complete. Thus for completed activities EV = PV and for an activity 50% complete then EV = PV/2. In the example below EV is below budget so the project is behind schedule. Actual costs (AC) are greater than EV so the project is over budget.

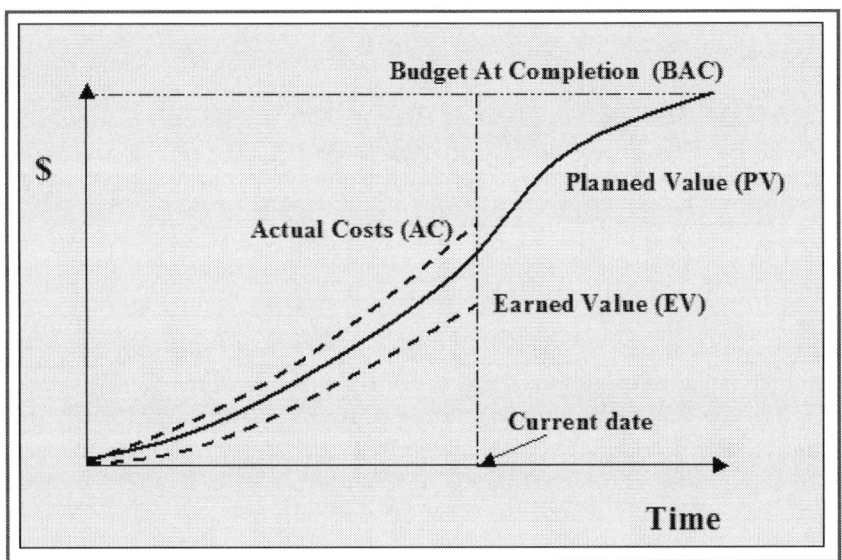

The point at which Actual Costs equal BAC, i.e. where all the budget is spent, is known as the **Point of Total Assumption**. This is because for a fixed price contract it is the point where the contractor assumes responsibility for all further costs.

4.3 Cost Performance Index (CPI)

CPI = EV/ AC

Example

I have done £250 worth of work (EV). The cost was £375 (AC).

Therefore the cost performance index = 250/375 = 0.67

(As a general rule experience shows that by the time 20% of a project has been completed the CPI is relatively stable)

4.4 Schedule Performance Index (SPI)

SPI = EV/ PV

Example

The value of the work done is £250 (EV).

The value of work scheduled (PV) is £500.

Therefore the schedule performance index is $250/500 = 0.5$

Note: CPI or SPI > 1 = positive outcome / ahead of schedule or budget
CPI or SPI < 1 = negative outcome / behind schedule or budget

4.5 Budget at Completion (BAC) or "Project Budget (PB)"

What was the total job supposed to cost? In our wall example it was £1000.

4.6 Forecasting

We can use the Earned Value information to forecast the project outcome at any point in the project.

Forecasting Cost

There are two different assumptions used to calculate Estimate Cost at Completion (EAC)

Assumption 1 assumes everything will be on plan from now on. We apply the formula:-

$$EAC = BAC - CV$$

In other words the current Cost Variance will be maintained until the end of the project.

Assumption 2 assumes that the remainder of the project will carry on with the same average efficiency so far. In this scenario:-

$$EAC = BAC/CPI \ \ (or \ PB/CPI)$$

Forecasting Time

This is not as straightforward as forecasting cost.

Assumption 1. Estimated Completion Date (ECD) = Current Planned Date + Slippage

Again this assumes that future work will be on plan, but how do we calculate slippage in terms of time? SV (Schedule Variance) is measured in money. The answer is that we use the earned value graph to convert money(SV) to time(slippage) as shown opposite.

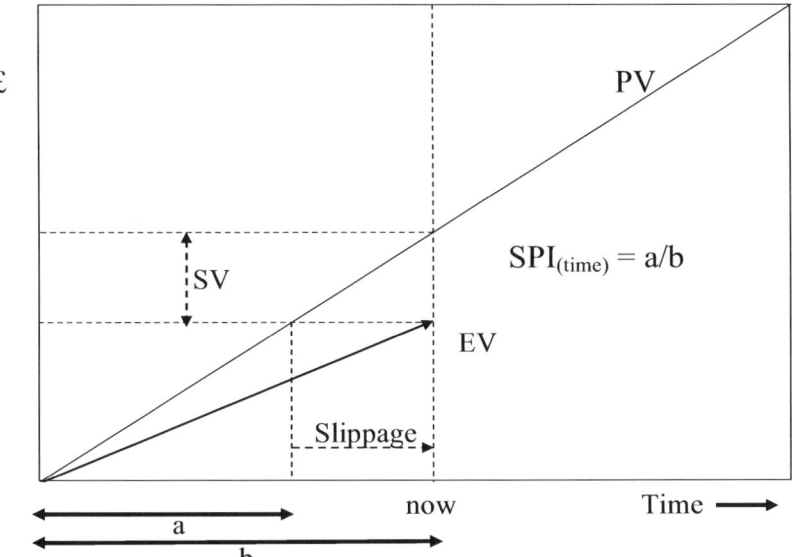

Assumption 2. Estimated Completion Date = Original Duration/SPI

This assumes that all remaining work will have the same SPI. Unfortunately this method can give misleading results especially towards the end of a project. This is because at the end of a project Earned Value approaches Planned Value and thus SPI approaches 1 regardless of performance. (The Earned Value can never exceed the Planned Value because once EV reaches PV then the work is complete)

To overcome this we calculate a new SPI called SPI $_{(time)}$ = A/B in the previous figure

Then Estimated Completion Date = Original Duration/ SPI $_{(time)}$

There remains the problem of deciding which assumption to use when forecasting. A project manager must justify whatever forecasting method is used. For instance if the current performance, for better or worse, has been caused by non repeatable circumstances, then assumption 1 is more appropriate. However if the current performance is due to factors which will continue to affect the project then it is appropriate to use assumption 2. Examples of such factors are overly optimistic or pessimistic estimates or labour performing much worse or better than expected. In many cases neither approach is applicable and it may be necessary to re-evaluate the project, especially if the original plan proves to be unrealistic.

In this case EAC = AC + ETC (Estimate to Complete)   i.e. Actuals to date + plus new estimate.

4.7 Variance at Completion   VAC = BAC – EAC

4.8 "To Complete Performance Index" TCPI

TCPI = $\dfrac{\text{Value of work remaining}}{\text{Value of budget remaining}}$

This determines the Cost Performance Index needed from now on, in order to complete the project to budget.

4.9 Requirements for Earned Value

In order for Earned Value to work the following elements need to be in place.

- A Work Breakdown Structure
- Assigned responsibilities for each task.
- Allocation of direct cost budget via the WBS
- All tasks scheduled
- A method of measuring achievement for each task
- Cost and achievement data collected at regular planned intervals
- A time phased budget baseline plan
- Baseline changes managed through change control

Note that non-productive activities such as management overheads, i.e. tasks that do not directly add value, are not normally included in EV calculations. Nor are major one off purchases such as capital equipment.

4.10 Earned Value Pros & Cons

Pros

- Focuses on useful work done not just on money/time spent
- Measures the whole project rather than concentrating on the Critical Path
- Allows us to forecast the project outcome using different assumptions
- Allows us to easily plot and monitor trends
- The requirement to measure real %age complete demands tighter control

Cons

- Because the technique takes a whole view, over-performance in 1 area may hide under-performance in another
- Slippage forecast based on SV is only valid if slippage applies to critical path
- It requires considerable administrative organisation & effort

4.11 Cash Flow

Cash Flow concerns the planning of project spending relative to income in such a way as to minimize the carrying cost of the financing for the project. For any project (or organisation) it is important to forecast and manage cash flow so as to ensure cash is available when needed. Companies manage cash flow by getting in debt as quickly as possible and by paying bills as late as possible.

Cost Accruals are for things that have been purchased but payment has not been made. Delaying payment improves cash flow.

Revenues can also be accrued. Sales are recognised (i.e. counted towards profit) when they are made, rather than when cash is received

Cash Flow is not the same as Profit/Loss. Companies trading at a profit can still go bust because of negative cash flow and vice versa.

4.12 Funding Limits

The organisation funding the project will typically set not just an overall project budget limit but will also attempt to control cash flow by imposing funding limits throughout the project. Such limits may cause activities to be delayed within the limits of float, or if the project is running over budget it may cause it to slow down to fit in with the funding limits.

5 Estimating Progress

5.1 The 50/50 rule

On a project with a large number of concurrent tasks it is often difficult to measure overall project progress as it is sometimes necessary to make subjective estimates for how far along we are on each task. The 50-50 rule was established to overcome this problem. When a task starts 50 percent of its PV is accounted for. On completion of the task the remaining 50 percent is charged. *This approach is only valid when all tasks are of similar order of magnitude and/or there are a large number of tasks and on average, current tasks are on plan.*

5.2 The 20/80 rule

This works in the same way but the estimate of Earned Value is more conservative.

5.3 The 0/100 rule

This is the most conservative rule. It is assumed that a task has no Earned Value until it is completed.

6 Financial Tools for Project Evaluation

6.1 Present Value

The key concept is that payment today is worth more than payment tomorrow.

Present value (PV) is the value today of future cash flows.

For a given future payment **t** years from now

$$PV = Mt / (1 + r)^t$$

Mt = amount of payment t years from now
r - interest rate (sometimes called "discount rate")
t - time period

Thus the Present Value of £1 in 2 years time at a discount rate of 10% = $1/(1.1)^2$ = 0.8264

Such values can be worked out for every year/discount rate combination.

The table below presents an analysis of present value **PV** with discount rate 10%. We can see that the Present Values for year 2 have been calculated by multiplying the cash flow value by the value calculated above. We apply the formulae to each annual cash flow and then add up all the resulting PVs to determine the NPV (Net Present Value). This represents the value of the project discounted to current values.

Year	Revenue £	Present Value (PV)	Cost £	Present Value (PV)	Total Present Value
0	0	0	50,000	50,000	-50,000
1	10,000	9.091	35,000	31,818	-22,727
2	20,000	16,529	15,000	12,397	4,132
3	30,000	22,539	5,000	3,757	18,783
4	40,000	27,321	5,000	3,415	23,905
5	50,000	31,046	5,000	3,105	27,941
	150,000	106,526	115,000	104,491	2.035

The point being made here is that a project that appears to be worth £35,000K (150 –115) is only worth £2,035 when discounted.

6.2 Internal Rate of Return (IRR)

We can use NPV to compare two or more projects. However such a straightforward comparison takes no account of the relative size of the projects. This problem is overcome by calculating the IRR. IRR is defined as that discount rate which makes the present value of costs equal to the present value of benefits. In the previous example if we had used an interest rate of 10.8% instead of 10% the Total Present Value would have been zero. Thus the IRR for this project is 10.8%.

6.3 Benefit-Cost Analysis

As the name implies this is a process that compares Benefits with Costs over the project life cycle. The ratio of the two values provides a measure of the expected profitability of a project and is called the Benefit/Cost ratio (or sometimes expressed the other way as a Cost/Benefit ratio.

Intangible Costs

Where costs can be directly measured in monetary terms the technique is very simple. Costs that cannot be measured this way are called Intangibles. An example of an intangible cost is the loss of quality of life due to a motorway being built near houses. An intangible benefit would be an improvement in village life due to the building of a by-pass.

6.4 Payback Period

This is the simplest of all the project evaluation tools but produces the least meaningful results. All this method does is to calculate how long it takes for cash flow to break even; i.e. when costs equal benefits. This method ignores cash flows after break-even point and also the changing value of money over time. It should only be used in together with other methods such as IRR.

6.5 Opportunity Cost

When an investment is made in a particular project then other investment opportunities have been passed over. Such possible returns, from competing opportunities are known as Opportunity Costs.

6.6 Sunk Cost

Sunk costs are money already spent or committed to, that cannot be recovered. Sunk costs should be ignored when making decisions about whether to continue investing in a continuing project. When adding up costs of a project then sunk costs must be included but for the purposes of investment decisions only future projected cash flows should be considered.

6.7 Variable Cost and Fixed Costs

Variable costs are those costs, which rise, in direct proportion to the size of the project, for example, the costs associated with labour.

Fixed costs are non-recurring expenses such as set-up costs or capital equipment.

6.8 Direct Costs and Indirect Costs

Direct costs are those costs, which can be attributed directly to the project. Typical items are project staff salaries, materials and 3rd party expenses.

Indirect costs are part of the owning organisation's overheads and are shared amongst all projects/departments. These costs include such things as facilities costs, utilities, management overhead etc.

6.9 Marginal Costs

The marginal cost of producing something is the extra cost associated with producing just 1 more item. All fixed costs are ignored.

7 Further Cost Management Terminology

7.1 Contingency Reserve

Contingency reserve is a pool of money held aside by the project manager to address problems that arise within the scope of work as defined by the WBS. Such problems are often referred to as known unknowns.

7.2 Management Reserve

Management reserve is a pool of money held aside to handle unforeseen problems that are unrelated to a specific work package. They are sometimes referred to as unknown-unknowns. They are usually not considered to be part of the project cost baseline.

7.3 Capital v. Revenue

All money spent on purchases is either Capital or Revenue. Money spent on assets or improvement to assets is called Capital. Such assets will have a value on the balance sheet and may be subject to depreciation. Money spent on consumable items required for the day to day running of the business is known as Revenue

7.4 Profit

Gross profit or sales profit or gross operating profit is the difference between sales revenue and the cost of making a product or providing a service, **before** deducting expenses (overhead, payroll, taxation, and interest payments).

Net Profit = gross profit less expenses

7.5 Depreciation of Capital

When money is spent to purchase capital equipment, its declining value, as it wears out, must be reflected on the balance sheet. This process is called depreciation. There are many methods of doing this and the choice is often arbitrary but must be justified to the auditors.

The straight-line method takes an equal credit during each year of the useful life of the equipment. Thus £1000 could be depreciated over say 5 years at £200/annum.
There are several methods for writing off the expense even faster than the straight-line approach (known as accelerated depreciation). Two of the common ones are as follows.

1. Double declining balance

In this method the largest depreciation is taken in the first year, typically double the value used for straight-line depreciation. At the end of each year the same %age of the amount outstanding is deducted from the remainder.

Thus for £1000 in Year 1 deduct 40% = £400   balance £600
In Year2 deduct 40% of £600   = £240   balance £360
In Year3 deduct 40% of £360   = £144   balance £216
In Year4 deduct 40% of £216   = £86   balance £130
In Year5 deduct 40% of £130   = £52   balance £78

At some predetermined time this process is terminated and all the balance written of otherwise the process would go on for infinity.

2. Sum of the years digits

This is best illustrated with an example. We wish to depreciate £1000 over 5 years.
We first sum the years digits.   i.e.   1+2+3+4+5=15

We then depreciate each year by dividing the years remaining by 15.

Thus Year1 = £1000 x 5/15 = £333
     Year2 = £1000 x 4/15 = £267
     Year3 = £1000 x 3/15 = £200
     Year4 = £1000 x 2/15 = £133
     Year5 = £1000 x 1/15 = <u>£ 67</u>

                 £1000

7.5 Value Analysis

In Value Analysis the design of an item is analysed to identify each of its functions as well as the cost of each function. Each function is then examined to see if it is justified by its cost, and whether it can be provided at a lower cost without degrading performance or quality.

7.6 Life-Cycle Cost (LCC)

Life Cycle in this context means total produce life. The life-cycle cost of an item or a system is the total cost of ownership of that item over its entire life cycle. This includes all cost from acquisition costs, through running costs to disposal costs. In a project environment the greater part of life cycle costs are often incurred after project completion. However the project team have a responsibility to bear total life cycle costs in mind when designing their solutions. There is no point in cutting project delivery costs if this results in an overall increase in life cycle costs.

7.7 Learning Curve

This is a graphical representation of the rather obvious principle that more times a task is carried out the better one gets at it. The learning curve shows the rate of improvement in performing a task as a function of time, or the rate of change in average cost as a function of cumulative output. In the initial stages the curve can be quite steep but eventually the rate of improvement slows down and levels off.

Budget Exercise Answer

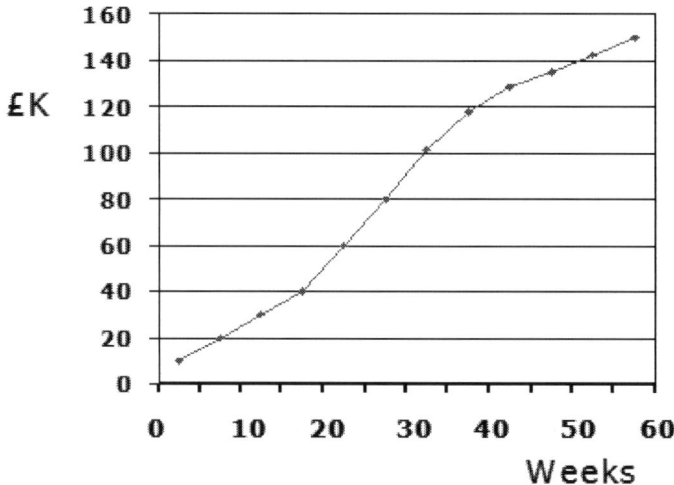

Cost Management Practice Questions

1. Estimate at completion (EAC) is computed by which of the following—

a. PV+AC
b. AC-EV
c. AC+ ETC
d. ETC+VAC

2. The direct cost of an activity is defined as the

a. Sum of all costs incurred
b. Sum of all the cost components that can be traced directly to the activity
c. Costs the project manager directed to be spent to accomplish the activity
d. Sum of all costs incurred minus profit

3. The most effective basis for determining the cost of a project is?

a. The Project Plan
b. The Scope Statement
c. The Cash Flow Statement
d. The Work Breakdown Structure

4. A "code of accounts" is a numbering system used to identify cost data for—

a. Each work package in the WBS
b. Tasks on a PERT chart
c. The company's account ledger
d. Each element of the WBS

5. Which of the following is not a recognised method of depreciation?

a. Year on year discounted value
b. Straight line approach
c. Double declining balance
d. Sum of the years digits

6. Which of the following budgets estimates represents the least accurate potential cost of a project?

a. Definitive estimate
b. Budget estimate
c. Life-cycle estimate
d. Order of magnitude estimate

7. A project will realise a benefit of $1 million in 2 years. With a prevailing interest rate of 10 percent. We must invest $0.41 million today to perform the work. The benefit/cost ratio is roughly-

a.   2:1
b.   4:1
c.   3.5:1
d.   1.5:1

8. Parametric modelling involves-

a.   Estimating the costs of individual work items, then summarising or rolling-up the individual estimates to get a project estimate
b.   Using the actual cost of a previous, similar project as the basis for estimating the cost of a current project
c.   Using project characteristics in a mathematical model to predict project costs
d.   The statistical sampling of a range of project costs to predict future costs

9. How is EAC calculated?

a. Divide project budget (PB) by the Schedule Performance Index (SPI)
b. Multiply PB by SPI
c. Multiply PB by the Cost Performance Index (CPI)
d. Divide PB by CPI

10. The budgeted cumulative cost curve represents—

a.   Planned cost of planned work
b.   Actual cost of work performed
c.   Budget at complete
d.   Variance at complete

11. If variable costs equal $200 per unit, and all fixed costs equal $1 600, what will be the cost of producing 10 units?

a. $600
b. $3600
c. $360
d. $4000

12. The Internal Rate of Return (IRR) for a project is?

a.   percentage profit
b.   The interest rate, which equates present values of costs and benefits.
c.   EAC - BAC
d.   Ratio of revenues to costs

13. Life-cycle costing is a concept that includes estimating the following costs in a project:

a. Acquisition, operating, and disposal costs
b. Direct, indirect, and general and administrative costs
c. Conceptual, planning, implementation, and closing costs
d. Planning and operating costs

14. Estimate at completion (EAC) is a periodic evaluation of the—

a. Cost of work completed
b. Value of work performed
c. Total cost at project completion
d. Forecasted cost of completion

15. A 12 month project has a budget at complete of $100,000. At month eight, actual costs were $104,000. What is the project status?

a. In trouble, since more was spent than was budgeted
b. Doing okay so far, since less was spent than was budgeted
c. There is not enough information to determine the status
d. Over budget and behind schedule

16. If EV 375, AC = 450, and PV = 325, what is the cost variance?

a. 25
b. -25
c. -75
d. -50

17. If EV = 350, AC = 450, and PV = 325, what is the schedule variance?

a. 25
b. -25
c. -75
d. -50

18. If EV 350, AC 400, and PV 325, what is the cost performance index?

a. 0.875
b. 1.078
c. 1.143
d. 0.081

19. What is (are) the most effective rule(s) for crashing a project?

a. Crash work packages with highest resource usage
b. Crash critical path
c. Crash tasks whose incremental cost of crashing is lowest
d. b and c

20. Which of the following techniques for cost estimating is considered the least accurate?

a. Analogous estimating
b. Parametric modelling
c. Bottom-up estimating
d. "Blue book"

21. The cumulative CPI has been shown to be relatively stable after what percentage of project completion?

a. 5%to10%
b. 15%to20%
c. 25%to35%
d. 50%to75%

22. Supporting detail for cost estimates should include all the following *except*—

a. A description of the scope of work
b. Documentation of the basis of the estimate and any assumptions made
c. An indication of the range of results
d. The number of people who participated in preparing the estimate

23. The budget held for "unknown unknowns" is part of the

a. Management reserve
b. Performance measurement baseline
c. Project reserve
d. Risk budget

24. The purpose of cost budgeting is to—

a. Determine the cost of the resources needed to complete project activities and allocate them to the proper chart of accounts for the organization
b. Monitor cost performance to detect variances from the plan
c. Allocate cost estimates to individual work items to establish a cost baseline against which project performance can be measured
d. Expend the minimum amount of funds possible

25. Cost Accounts

a. Are charge accounts for personnel time management
b. Summarize project costs at level 2 of the WBS
c. Identify and track management reserves
d. Represent the basic level at which project performance is measured and reported

26. Which of the following calculations cannot be used to determine EAC?

a. Earned Value to date plus the remaining project budget
b. Actuals to date plus a new estimate for all remaining work
c. Actuals to date plus the remaining budget
d. Actuals to date plus the remaining budget modified by a performance factor

27. Which of the following is a definition of Gross Profit?

a. The difference between sales revenue and the cost of making a product or providing a service, before deducting expenses
b. The difference between sales revenue and the cost of making a product or providing a service, after deducting expenses
c. Total profit before payment of taxes
d. Total profit less tax, interest and dividends

28. According to learning curve theory, when many items are produced repetitively—

a. Production equipment that requires less operator training lowers unit costs
b. Unit costs decrease as production rates increase
c. Unit costs decrease as more units are produced
d. Costs of training increase as the level of automation increases

29. The process of cost control includes all the following actions except—

a. Monitoring cost performance to detect variances from the plan and determining the reasons for both positive and negative variances
b. Selecting projects using IRR, present value, or other techniques to ensure profitability
c. Preventing incorrect, inappropriate, or unauthorized changes from being included in the cost baseline
d. Ensuring that all appropriate changes are recorded accurately in the cost baseline

30. Financial analysis of payback period identifies the

a. Ratio of discounted revenues over discounted costs
b. Future value of money invested today
c. Amount of time before net cash flow becomes positive
d. Point in time where costs exceed profit

31. The method of calculating the EAC by dividing the project budget by the cost performance index is appropriate when---

a. Current variances are viewed as atypical ones
b. Original estimating assumptions are no longer reliable because conditions have changed
c. Current and past variances are viewed as typical of future variances
d. Original estimating assumptions are considered to be fundamentally flawed

32. Which of these represents earned value in terms of effort?

a. Actual effort hours
b. Useful effort hours
c. Estimated effort hours
d. Cost of effort hours

33. A resource-limited project is one in which—

a. Functional managers do not allocate the required number of resources at the time required by the project manager
b. The project must be finished as soon as possible but without exceeding a specific level of resource usage
c. The project must be finished by a certain time using as few resources as possible
d. The resources assigned to the project are limited in their ability to perform

34. The Point of Total Assumption is when---

a. The project manager assumes full control of the project
b. The project is formally handed over to the client
c. Actual costs equal the project budget
d. None of the above

35. Opportunity cost is defined as the cost of—

a. The cost of bidding and winning a project opportunity
b. Preparing proposals in response to a buyer's project requirements
c. Performing all marketing and business development activities
d. The potential profit lost from opportunities not taken up

36. Which of the following would you not put under Earned Value control?

a. Project team wages and salaries
b. Equipment hire
c. Capital equipment purchases
d. Utilities

PRACTICE QUESTION ANSWERS

		Page	**Paragraph**	
1	C	90	4.6	
2	B	95	6.8	
3	D	84	2.3	The WBS is the basis of most things
4	D	43	4.1	
5	A	96	7.5	
6	D	85	2.6	
7	A	94	6.1	The present value of $1M in 2 years is $0.826M. Compared with $0.41 investment this give a ratio of 2:1
8	C	85	2.4	
9	D	90	4.5	
10	A	86	3.0	
11	B	95	6.7	10 x 200 + 1,600 = 3,600
12	B	94	6.2	
13	A	97	7.6	
14	D	90	4.5	
15	A	90	4.5	All we know for certainty is that we have exceeded the budget. We have no information on the schedule.
16	C	88	4.1	CV = EV- AC = 375 - 450 = -75
17	A	88	4.1	SV = EV - PV = 350 - 325 = 25
18	A	89	4.3	CPI = EV/AC = 350/400 = 0.875
19	D	65	3.10	
20	A	84	2.1	
21	B	89	4.3	
22	D	85	2.6	a), b) and c) should all be documented but d) is not relevant
23	A	95	7.2	
24	C	85	3.0	More than 1 answer seems reasonable here but c) is the *best* answer
25	D	84	2.3	
26	A	90	4.6	In order to forecast the total expenditure you need to know the actuals to date.
27	A	96	7.4	
28	C	98	7.7	Learning curve is about total number of units produced and not the rate of production
29	B	82	1.3	
30	C	95	6.4	
31	C	90	4.6	
32	B	87	4.0	
33	B	67	3.11	
34	C	89	4.2	
35	D	95	6.5	
36	C	92	4.9	

Chapter 6

Project Quality Management

1 Quality Management Processes

Project Quality management consists of those processes required to ensure that the project will satisfy the needs for which it was undertaken. The major processes are:-

1.1 Plan Quality

This involves determining what quality standards are appropriate for the project and then producing a Quality Plan which documents how to achieve them.

1.2 Perform Quality Assurance

Quality Assurance encompasses those activities necessary to ensure that the Quality Plan is being adhered to and as such can be though of as an audit function.

1.3 Perform Quality Control

Quality Control is concerned with the physical monitoring and measurement of project outputs and deliverables to ensure that they comply with the planned standards

What follows is a description of the key concepts underlying these processes.

2 Key Quality Concepts

2.1 Customer Expectations

The *PMBOK® Guide* emphasises the growing attention to customer requirements as the basis for managing quality. A "Quality Product" is one that satisfies customer requirements in terms of compliance to specification. Compliance to specification also means avoidance of "gold-plating." Simply defined, gold-plating is giving the customer more than what was required. Exceeding the specified requirements is a waste of time and money, with no value added to the project. The customer should expect and receive exactly what was specified-no more, no less. This is the underlying philosophy of project quality management espoused by PMI.

2.2 Definition of Quality

Modern thinking on Quality defines it as meeting mutually agreed-upon customer needs and expectations." The *PMBOK® Guide* defines it more formally as:-

"The degree to which a set of inherent characteristics fulfil requirements"

This infers conformance to requirements/specifications and fitness for purpose.

2.3 Quality v Grade

Do not confuse Quality with Grade. For instance a piece of software can be low grade and high quality. i.e. contains only basic features but is bug free and well documented. Or it can be high grade and low quality i.e. rich in features but full of bugs and badly documented.

2.4 The 5 Quality Principles

1. Teamwork
2. Commitment to World Class Standards
3. Customer Focused
4. Continuous Improvement
5. Process Oriented (Prevention not Correction)

2.5 Five Key Messages

1. Quality does not mean Luxury: A Rolls Royce that conforms to the requirements for a Rolls Royce is a quality car. However a Lada that conforms to the requirements for a Lada is also a quality car

2. Quality is tangible and measurable: Quality can be measured as the cost of quality. Crosby defines cost of quality as the expense of non-conformance, i.e. the cost of doing things wrong. He enlarges the concept by including the actions associated with prevention.

3. Quality is not a luxury; This view mistakenly associates quality with luxury and assumes adding "quality" is often too expensive. It is always cheaper to do things right first time

4. Quality problems start with management: Reducing the cost of quality is largely under the control of management.

5. Quality is not just a function of the Quality department: Quality problems originate all over the organisation. Quality is the business of everyone.

2.6 Crosby's 4 Absolutes of Quality

1. Conformance to requirements

2. Quality comes from prevention

3. The standard to aim for is zero defects

4. The cost of Quality can be measured

2.7 Prevention over Inspection

The time to fix quality problems is during design and planning and not after manufacture. Quality is built in not inspected in.

2.8 Acceptable Quality Level

It used to be thought that quality problems are inevitable and that a certain level of defects is acceptable. The modern approach to quality is that there is no such thing as an Acceptable Quality Level. The aim should always be zero defects.

3 Quality Management

Quality management is a management discipline concerned with making sure that activities happen according to a prescribed plan. It is all about preventing problems. The PMBOK® *Guide* defines Quality management as carrying out a project through its four phases (concept, development, execution, and finish) with zero deviations from the project specifications.

The 3 main processes comprising Project Quality Management are:-

1. Plan Quality
2. Perform Quality Assurance
3. Perform Quality Control

3.1 Plan Quality

The *PMBOK® Guide* defines quality planning as "identifying which quality standards are relevant to the project and determining how to satisfy them" The primary output of the quality planning process is the Project Quality Management Plan. This describes how the project team intends to implement its Quality Policy. This reinforces the basis of modern thinking about project quality management; that is quality is a planned activity and not something that is applied afterwards by inspection and correction. Inspection still has a part to play in quality management; however increased inspection is not generally considered the best path to improved quality.

3.2 Perform Quality Assurance

The *PMBOK® Guide* defines Quality Assurance as the process of evaluating overall project performance on a regular basis to provide confidence that the project will satisfy the relevant quality standards. The following items are part of quality assurance:

Audit

This is the process of reviewing specific data at appropriate points within the project's life cycle so as to allow stakeholders to obtain knowledge as to how the project is proceeding, and to determine if any corrective actions are necessary

Post Project Review

The objective is to learn lessons that can be applied to future projects. This is not just about recording things that went wrong but also noting things that went well.

Ownership of Quality Responsibility

Management has overall accountability for Quality Policy and Standards across the whole organisation. The PM is accountable for project quality and quality outcome for product delivered – within the framework of the quality policies set by management. Each individual is accountable for the quality of the work they have been assigned, but only in so far as they have been provided with clear guidelines on the quality expectation and that they have been adequately trained to complete the work to a quality standard.

The ultimate responsibility for quality lies with the individual person who is performing the task.

Cost of Quality

Kerzner distinguishes between the Cost of Conformance and Cost of Non-conformance as follows.

Costs of conformance (proactive)

- Training
- Indoctrination
- Verification
- Validation
- Testing
- Audits
- Maintenance
- Calibration

Cost of non-conformance (failure)

- Scrap
- Rework
- Warranty repairs
- Complaint handling
- Product recalls
- Lost future business

Costs of failure are sometimes split into internal costs e.g. scrap, downtime, and external costs e.g Warranty, loss of future business

Deming says that at least 85 percent of the costs of poor quality are the direct responsibility of management.

3.3 Perform Quality Control

Quality control is a technical function which is involved with the process of monitoring specific project /product parameters to determine if they comply with relevant quality standards. Quality control in a product environment is very much a statistical process.

4 Statistics for Quality Control

4.1 Sampling

Sampling is used to assess the properties of a population when examining the whole population is not feasible. There are two main types of sampling, variable and attribute.

4.2 Variable Sampling

This is defined as a characteristic that is measured over a range of values. Examples are diameter measured in inches, cooking time measured in minutes, and weight measured in pounds. This is the basis of Control Charts (see later)

4.3 Attribute Sampling

Attribute sampling is a quality characteristic that is classified as either conforming, or non-conforming to specifications or requirements. There is no middle ground. Normally an acceptance limit is set for a "sample" taken from a "lot" or "batch". e.g in a lot of 10,000 components 100 are selected at random. If say there are 2 or more failures then the entire batch is rejected or sometimes subjected to retest. With all sampling there is a risk that the wrong result will be obtained .i.e. accepting a bad batch or rejecting an acceptable batch.

4.4 Probability

The fundamental concept in quality control is that of probability. Probability is about ascribing numeric values to the chance that something will happen. For example, in flipping a coin there is a 50 percent chance (or probability) of correctly calling heads or tails. When throwing a six sided die the probability of correctly forecasting the number thrown is 1/6.

4.5 Statistical Independence

Statistical events that are unaffected by the outcome of other events are said to be independent. e.g throws of a die, tosses of a coin.

4.6 Probability Distributions

For variables, probability is a more complicated concept. We measure the occurrences of an event or characteristic, and distribute them over the entire range of the characteristic. Such a distribution is called a probability distribution.

An example of a simple probability distribution is the measurement of the probability of throws from a pair of dice, shown in opposite. This type of depiction is called a histogram.

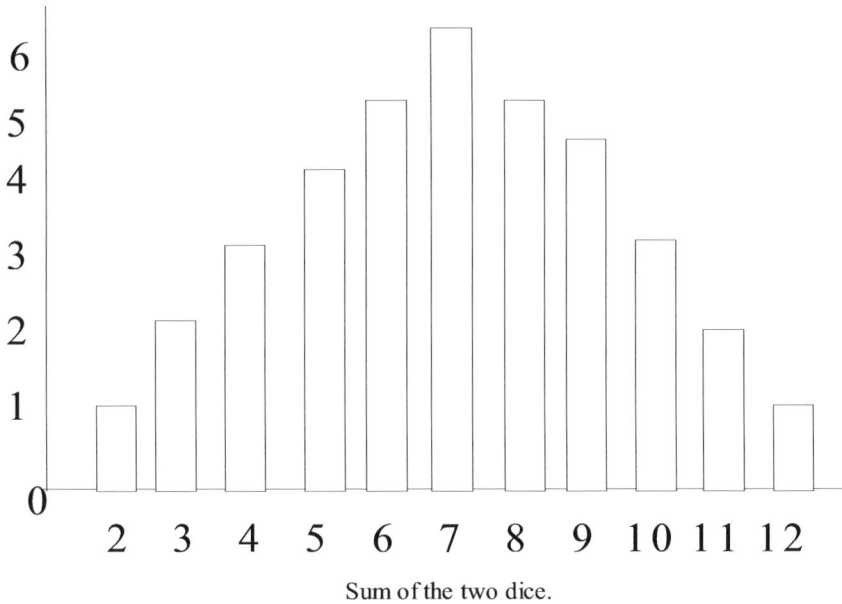

Number of ways the dice
could add up to a given number.

Sum of the two dice.

4.7 The Normal Distribution

In the above example the possible values from the throw of 2 dice are discrete numbers. An example of a distribution where the possible values are continuous is the Normal Distribution. (See figure below)

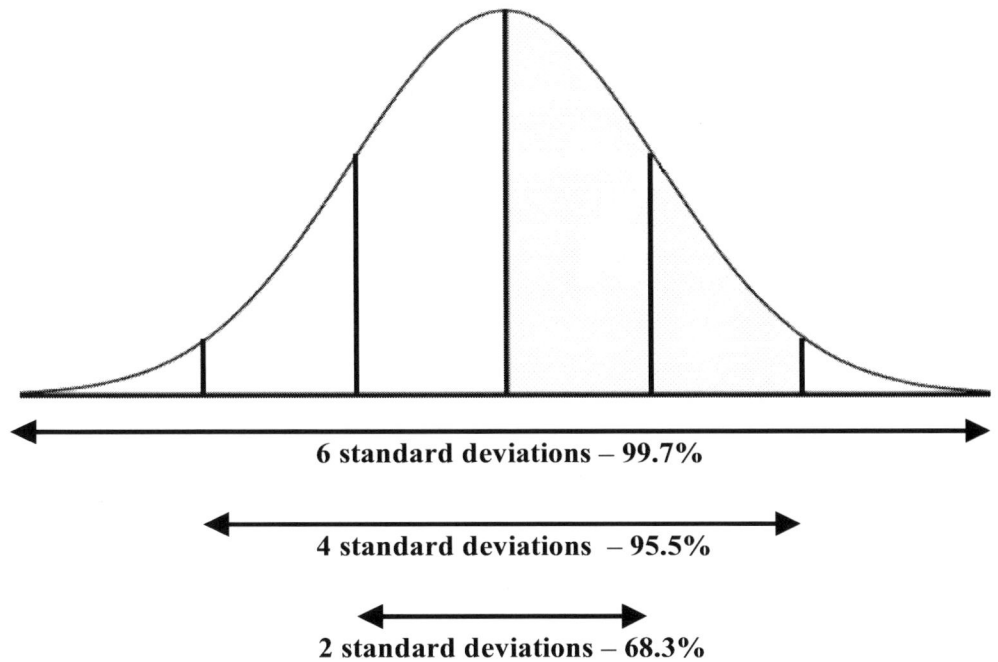

6 standard deviations – 99.7%

4 standard deviations – 95.5%

2 standard deviations – 68.3%

This probability distribution has a bell shape and is symmetric about its mean; it is known as a Normal distribution or a bell curve. It is called normal because there are many examples of it occurring in nature. The term, standard deviation is explained overleaf.

4.8 Measures of Central Tendency

The three terms Mean, Median and Mode are collectively known as measures of central tendency. The Mean is well known, being the statistical term for Average. The Median and Mode are less well known but are both simple concepts that could be tested in the PMI exam.

The Median of a distribution is the middle value. Thus in the list of values 10,10,20,30,60,80.90 the middle value, and hence the Median, is 30.

If there are an even number of values we take the mean of the middle two. Thus in the list of values 10,20,30,60,80,90 the Median is the mean of 30 and 60 i.e. 45.

The Mode is the most popular value. In a histogram it would be the value of the highest bar. For a continuous distribution it is the highest point of the curve. A typical question could be;
what is the Mode of the following list of values? 10,10,20,30,40,40,40,50.

 The answer is 40, it being the most popular value. If no number is most popular then there is no Mode.

Note that for the Normal Distribution the Mean, Mode and Median all coincide. This is because the Normal distribution is symmetrical about the mean. For distributions that are skewed the values will differ.

4.9 Standard Deviation (a measure of spread)

In measuring samples and comparing them to their overall population, one important concept is that of standard deviation. Simply defined, the standard deviation is the amount on either side of the mean of a normal distribution that will contain approximately 68.3 percent of the total population. The amount within two standard deviations will include 95.5 percent, and within three standard deviations will include 99.7 percent of the population. This is illustrated in 4.7.

We use the character sigma, σ, to denote the standard deviation of an entire population.
In order to estimate the standard deviation of a population we take a sample from that population. This estimated standard deviation is called the sample standard deviation and is denoted by S.

Application to PERT-The Beta Distribution

When using PERT we estimate the expected value for the duration of an activity as:-

$\mu = (o + 4m + p)/6$

Where p = pessimistic, o = optimistic and m = most likely.

When working with PERT estimates there is a very simple way to approximate the standard deviation of an activity.. The standard deviation is approximated by the formulae:-

$\sigma = (p - o)/6$

The distribution underlying this equation is the Beta Distribution below.

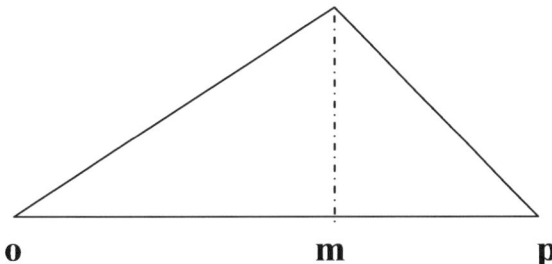

o   m   p

A similar technique can be used for any list of numbers. Deduct the smallest from the biggest and divide by 6. The answer will at least give an order of magnitude that can often identify the correct answer from a multiple choice list.

Another statistic you need to be aware of is Variance V

Note: (This is a statistical term and is not to be confused with the variance used in finance and scheduling (plan - actual))

The Variance of a distribution is Standard Deviation squared. $V = \sigma^2$

Variances are additive. This property can be used to answer questions such as the following:-

A 2 stage manufacturing process has a standard deviation for process 1 where $\sigma 1 = 3$, and for process 2 , $\sigma 2 = 4$. What is the standard deviation of the overall process?

Answer: $V = \sigma^2$

$\therefore V1 = \sigma 1^2 = 9$ and $V2 = \sigma 2^2 = 16$

 $V = V1 + V2 = 9 + 16 = 25$ (Because Variances are additive)

$\therefore \sigma^2 = 25$ $\therefore \sigma = 5$

4.10 Applying the Normal Distribution

Example1: A Monte Carlo simulation of a project schedule suggests that it is expected to complete in 8 weeks with a standard deviation of 2 weeks. What is the probability of it completing in 10 weeks or less?

To answer this we need the following diagram. The values are derived from those in the figure of paragraph 4.7.

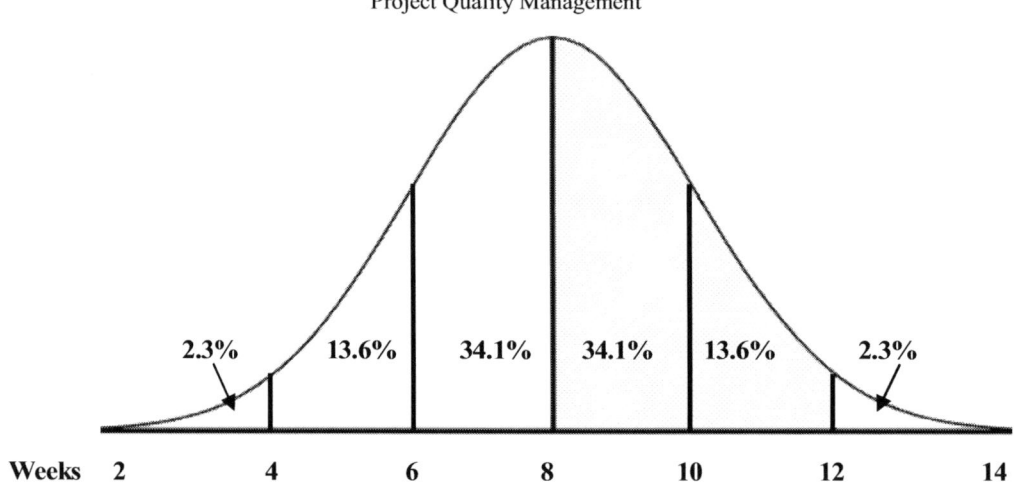

Project Quality Management

Answer = 84% (i.e area under curve to left of 10 weeks = 2.3+13.6+ 34.1+34.1)

Example 2: The estimated cost of a project is $1,000,000 with a standard deviation of $50,000. If the budget has been set at $1,100,000 what is the probability of going over budget?

Answer: The budget is set at $100,000 more than the estimated cost. This equates to 2 standard deviations. Thus the probability of going over by more than 2 standard deviations is represented by the area under the curve beyond 2 standard deviations from the mean i.e. 2.3%

4.11 Elementary Probability Theory

Two electrical components have failure rates of 1% and 5% respectively

a) If two are wired in parallel what is the probability of total failure?

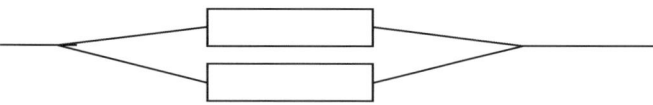

Answer a)

For total failure both must fail.

Probability of failure = .01 x .05 = .0005

b) If two are wired in series what is the probability of total failure?

Answer b)

For total failure only 1 need fail. i.e. both must succeed.

Probability of success = 1 – Probability of failure

Probability of both succeeding = (1- .01) x (1- .05) =   .99 x .95 = .9405

Therefore Probability of total failure = 1- .9405 = .0595

It can be seen that a) is much more reliable than b) This illustrates the principle of Redundancy.

Probability theory can also be applied to Risk Analysis (see Chapter 9)

5 Quality Control Tools

5.1 Flow Charts

Flowcharts are an important quality control tool as they allow design faults to be discovered before committing to build by depicting process flows and the inputs and outputs of processes.

5.2 Pareto Charts

In the 19th century an Italian economist called Vilfredo Pareto found that typically 80 percent of the wealth in a region was concentrated in less than 20 percent of the population. This was taken up in modern times by Dr. Joseph Juran who formulated what he called the Pareto Principle. This states that in most situations only a vital few elements (20 percent) account for the majority (80 percent) of the problems that are occurring. For example take an automobile production line. It has been shown that 20% of the possible causes account for 80 percent of the downtime. The practical application of the Pareto principle is that 80% of the problems can be cured by addressing only 20% of the causes.

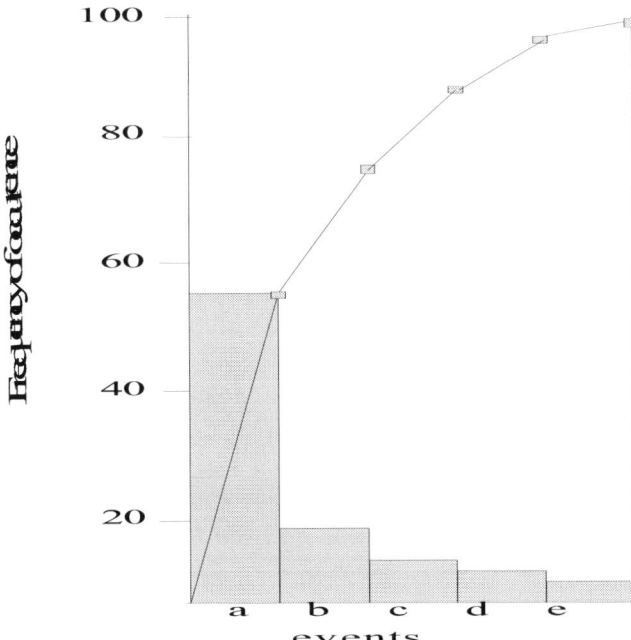

A Pareto Chart is a bar chart in which the data are arranged in descending order of their importance, generally by magnitude of frequency, cost, time, or a similar parameter. The chart presents the information being examined in its order of priority and focuses attention on the most critical issues.

5.3 Cause & Effect Diagrams (also called Fishbone or Ishikawa diagrams)

The cause-and-effect diagram of which a typical example is shown below, is a useful tool to represent relationships among a list of items or factors. It is extremely useful as a brainstorming tool. The construction of a cause-and-effect diagram, particularly when done as a group activity, stimulates ideas and facilitates the unearthing of all possible causes and effects. The process is also self-documenting.

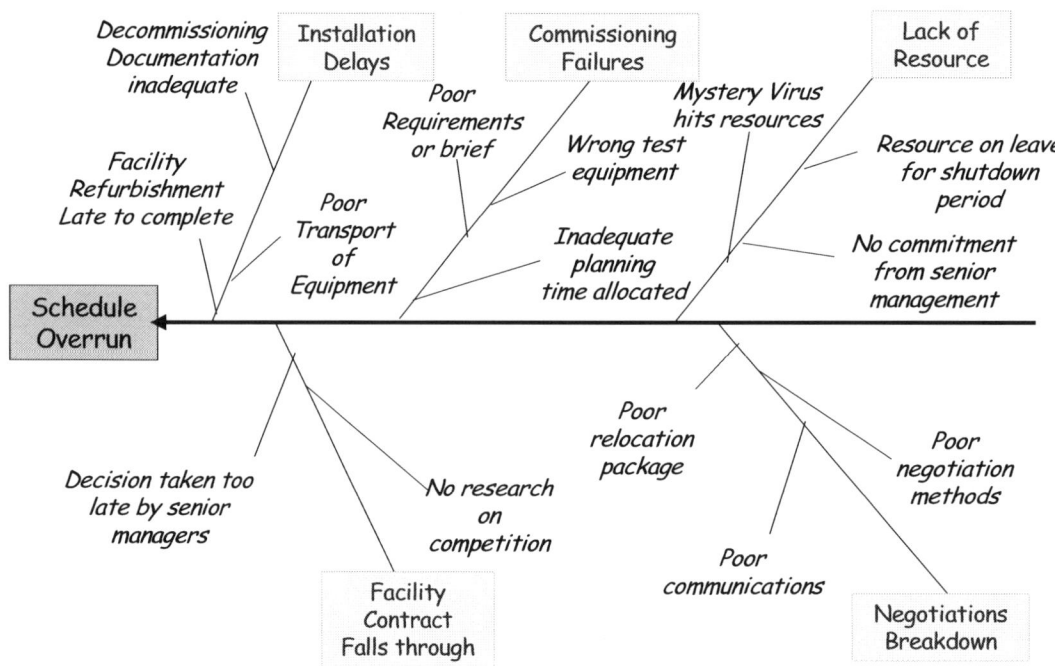

5.4 Control Charts

A control chart (opposite, top) is a graph that displays data taken over time. They are sometimes called Shewhart Charts. Control charts are used to show the variation of a process so as to allow you to distinguish between measurements that are predictably within the inherent capability of the process (normal causes of variation that are to be expected) and measurements that are unpredictable and produced by special causes.

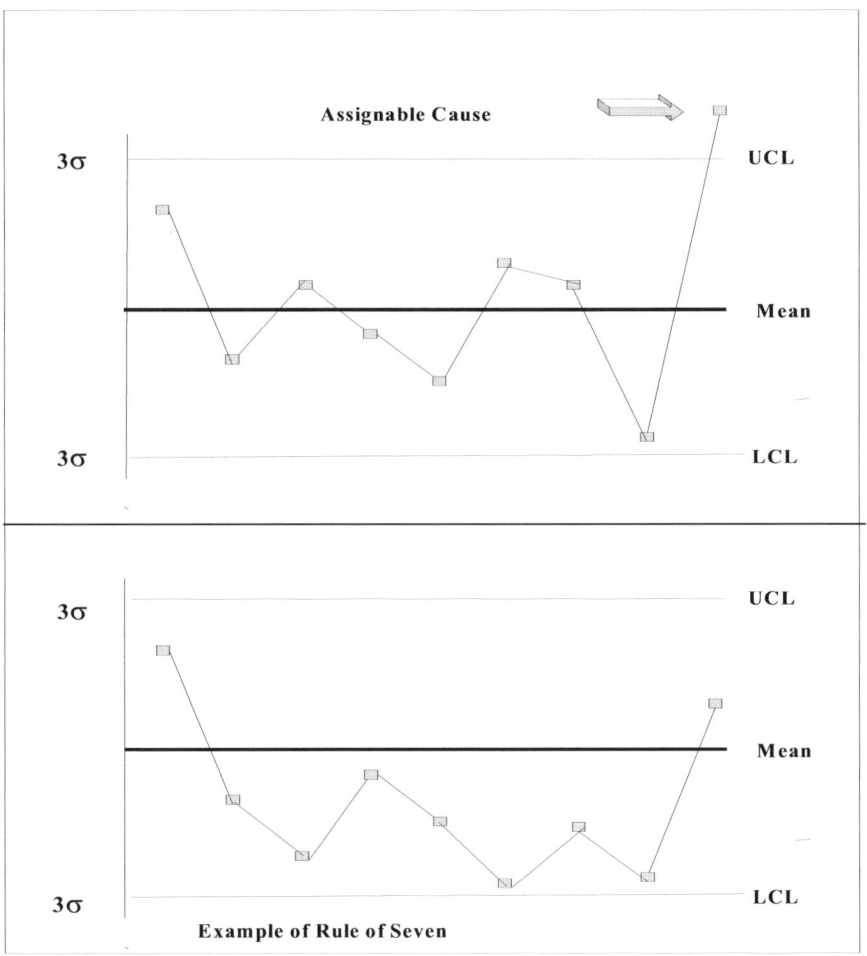

Control Limits

The centre line of the chart represents the process average or mean. The upper and lower control limits (UCL & LCL) are typically set at 3sigma either side of the mean. This means that for a Normal distribution 99.7% of values will be within the control limits. Thus a value outside these limits is highly likely to indicate a problem with the process.

Control limits describe the natural variation of the process such that points within the limits are generally indicative of normal and expected variation. Points outside the limits signal that probably something has occurred that requires special attention because it is outside of the built-in systemic causes of variation in the process.

A control chart without limits is known as a Run Chart.

Assignable Causes

It is possible that points outside the 3σ control limits are due to random variation. However it is likely that there is an assignable cause, meaning that their occurrence may be the result of unwanted, external effects such as-
An equipment problem
An employee problem (poor training, understaffed etc)
Defective materials

Specification Limits

The upper and lower control limits (UCL and LCL) must not be confused with specification limits. Specification limits (or tolerances) can often be more stringent than the capability of the process. It may be that for say jet engine components the tolerance may be equal to a lot less than 3 sigma. If the process can not be improved to reduce its inherent variation then a large proportion of the production will be rejected (this is the case in computer chip production). However in this instance the process is still under control if it is within control limits and obeying the rule of 7 (below). Thus a process in control can still produce out of spec goods.(see 5.5)

Rule of 7

There is another important guideline, known as the Rule of Seven, which should be observed whenever using control charts. This rule of thumb (heuristic) states that if seven or more observations in a row occur on the same side of the mean (even though they may be within the control limit) or if seven or more readings show a continuous upward or downward trend they should be investigated as if they had an assignable cause. It is extremely unlikely that seven observations in a row would be on the same side of the mean if the process is operating normally. (Such a situation is illustrated in the lower chart in the previous figure.)

If a process is operating normally, the observations will follow a random pattern with some of the points falling above the line and some below the line. In fact, the probability that any single point will fall above or below the line is 50-50 (like a coin toss). Further, the probability that seven points in a row would be on the same side of the line would be calculated as $(1/2)6 = 1/64$). This rule provides a guideline that alerts you that something unlikely is happening and you should check it out. These charts will help you understand the inherent capability of your processes, bring your processes under control by eliminating the special causes of variation, reduce tampering with processes that are under statistical control, and monitor the effects of process changes aimed at improvement.

Effect of Sample Size

If instead of taking a single sample at any moment in time we take several and use the average value, then this will have the effect of reducing the variability of our readings. Thus the larger the sample size the smaller will be the standard deviation of the control values. For a sample of size N the control value will be reduced by a factor of $\sqrt{N}$. Thus the control limits must be set in conjunction with the sample size. A large sample size will result in lower standard deviation and hence tighter control limits and vice versa.

5.5 Process Capability Index

One additional concept is important in the use of control charts, namely the Process Capability Index.

This index relates the Specification limits to the Control limits.

Cp is called the Inherent Process Capability Index
Cp = (Upper spec limit - lower spec limit)/ 6 x sigma
Thus if a component has a specification of 12" plus or minus .015" and the process which manufactures it produces parts with a standard deviation of .002 then

Cp = (12.015 - 11.985)/(6 x .002) =.03/.012 = 2.5

This means that the process is well capable of producing parts that are well within tolerance. In this case the process may be too good. (gold plating). An index of 1 means that the tolerance range is exactly 6 sigma and hence 99.7% of components are within specification.

The Voice of the Customer   ⟶   What the Customer requires

The Voice of the Process   ⟶   What the Process delivers

The optimum performance is reached when the Voice of the Process equals the Voice of the Customer.

6   Further Quality Concepts

6.1 Continuous Improvement and Kaizen

Toyota pioneered the concept of Continuous Improvement. They demonstrated that small, incremental, ongoing improvements to Quality can be more effective than large disruptive changes.

The Japanese word for continuous improvement is **Kaizen**. The philosophy espoused by kaizen is that quality comes from continuous minor improvements. It is the responsibility of both workers and management to always be on the look out for ways to improve the quality of the finished product and the processes that produce it. However the process has to be driven from the top.

Another Japanese word that is associated with continuous improvement is "**Warusa-kagen**,". This refers to things that are not yet giving rise to quality problems, but have the potential for doing so and if not fixed could develop into serious problems.

6.2 Benchmarking

Most major companies aspire to become "World Class" or "Best in Class". To do this it is necessary to compare practices and products with those of other companies in order to set Benchmarks to measure yourself against.

6.3 Just-in-Time (JIT) and Kanban

Kanban stands for Kan- card, Ban- signal. The essence of the Kanban concept is that a supplier or the warehouse should only deliver components to the production line as and when they are needed, i.e. Just-in-Time, so that there is no storage in the production area. Within this system, workstations located along production lines only produce/deliver desired components when they receive a card and an empty container, indicating that more parts will be needed in production. Since Kanban is a chain process in which orders flow from one process to another, the production or delivery of components is pulled to the production line. In contrast to the traditional forecast oriented method where parts are pushed to the line.

When there is no safety stock in the system, defective parts or processes will result in lost production. JIT thus forces a company to find and fix quality problems before they occur.

6.4 Priority of Quality versus Cost and Schedule

Modern thinking emphasises that quality shares at least equal priority with cost and schedule but what is most important will depend on the nature of the project. When these 3 parameters become mutually incompatible, which commonly occurs, it is the responsibility of the client or sponsor to decide which is most important. It is the job of the project manager to quantify the problem and point out the options.

6.5 Impacts of Poor Quality

The following effects on a project are possible results of poor quality:

- Increased project costs as a result of costs of non-conformance, for example, rework, scrap, product recalls, and so on.
- Decreased productivity
- Increased risk and uncertainty (less predictability in cost, schedule, and technical outcomes).
- Increased costs of monitoring (if conformance to specs is low, increased monitoring will probably become necessary)

6.6 Design and Quality

Quality should be designed in; not inspected in. More specifically, careful design of a product or service is believed to increase reliability and maintainability (two important measures of quality).

6.7 Deming

Deming is another guru who may come up in the exam. Deming defines quality as:--
"Continuous improvement of products and services." You should also memorise what Deming calls his 4 step Cycle for Improvements:-

Plan> Identify problem and develop improvement plan

Do> Implement the plan on a test basis

Check> See if desired results are being achieved

Act> Implement corrective actions

Repeat Cycle

6.8 The Juran Trilogy

One of the established Gurus in the quality world is Juran. He has coined, and even trademarked, what he calls the Juran Trilogy. For Juran, Quality is built on the three processes:-

1. Quality Planning
2. Quality Control
3. Quality Improvement

6.9 Quality Function Deployment (QFD)

QFD helps a design team to define, design, manufacture and deliver a product or service to meet customer's needs. In QFD the product should always be designed to meet the needs of the ultimate end user. Its main feature is to capture the requirements and ensure they are met by cross-functional teamwork across the project phases. (Related to concurrent engineering)

6.10 The Taguchi Method

This is a statistical technique used to estimate the cost associated with failure to control process variability. Its principle is that by paying more attention to design then products can be produced that are more forgiving or tolerant to process variations

6.11 ISO 9000

ISO 9000 is an official framework for Quality Systems recognised worldwide. It provides a basic set of requirements for a quality system without being industry specific and without specifying means of implementation.

6.12 Total Quality Management (TQM)

TQM is not a quality technique. It is a philosophy concerned with how best to achieve quality improvement within an organisation, bringing together the approaches of Deming, Juran and Crosby. It is an approach that puts quality at the heart of everything that it done by the organisation. It lays particular stress on meeting customer needs and expectations and encompassing all parts of the organisation.

6.13 Six Sigma

Six sigma literally means 3.4 defects per million. In practice it is a methodical approach to improving process quality that aims for zero defects. It was first developed by MOTOROLA in the eighties but is now widely practiced.

Six Sigma projects follow two project methodologies inspired by Deming's Plan-Do-Check-Act Cycle.

1) DMAIC is used for projects aimed at improving an existing business process

2) DMADV is used for projects aimed at creating new product or process designs

DMAIC

- **Define** high-level project goals and the current process.
- **Measure** key aspects of the current process and collect relevant data.

- **Analyze** the data to verify cause-and-effect relationships.
- **Improve** or optimize the process based upon data analysis.
- **Control** to ensure that any deviations from target are corrected before they result in defects.

First Time Yield (FTY):

The proportion of production that goes through a production process without requiring rework.

Rolled Throughput Yield (RTY):

Applies to a series of processes and is the product of all the individual FTYs.

DMADV

- **Define** design goals that are consistent with customer demands and corporate strategy.
- **Measure** and identify CTQs (characteristics that are **Critical To Quality**), product capabilities, production process capability, and risks.
- **Analyze** to develop and design alternatives, create a high-level design and evaluate design capability to select the best design.
- **Design** details, optimize the design, and plan for design verification. This phase may require simulations.
- **Verify** the design, set up pilot runs, implement the production process and hand it over to the process owners.

DMADV is also known as DFSS, "Design For Six Sigma".

Six Sigma identifies several key roles for its successful implementation.

- *Executive Leadership* includes the CEO and other members of top management.
- *Champions* are responsible for Six Sigma implementation across the organization in an integrated manner.
- *Master Black Belts*, identified by champions, act as in-house coaches on Six Sigma. They devote 100% of their time to Six Sigma.
- *Black Belts* operate under Master Black Belts to apply Six Sigma methodology to specific projects. They devote 100% of their time to Six Sigma.
- *Green Belts* are the employees who take up Six Sigma implementation along with their other job responsibilities. They operate under the guidance of Black Belts.

6.14 Design of Experiments (DOE)

When trying to improve quality in a process we can vary certain parameters and measure the change in quality. There are often a large number of factors of which some will be out of our control. Many factors can interact with each other and either reinforce or negate each other. It is thus often very difficult to identify and isolate the effects of different factors. Design of Experiments is a body of statistical techniques that can provide a framework for determining an optimum set of conditions for a process by determining what the key factors are and how they interact.

6.15 Concurrent Engineering

Concurrent Engineering is a systematic approach to the integrated, concurrent design of products and their related processes, including, manufacturing and support. The essence of this approach is that instead of each function completing their part of the project and then passing it on, all functions co-operate. For instance the product designers will involve the manufacturing department to make sure that what they design can be efficiently manufactured and is maintainable. As well as reducing the time taken to develop a product by reducing the need for corrective iterations it also improves quality.

Quality Management Practice Questions

1. The "rule of seven" as applied to statistical process control charts means-

a. There are typically seven rejects per thousand inspections.
b. There are seven consecutive points that are ascending, descending, or on the same side of the mean
c. At least seven measurements must be taken in order for the process to be validated.
d. A process is not out-of-control notwithstanding that seven measurements fell outside the LCL and UCL.

2. Specifying an acceptable quality level (AQL) is inconsistent with modern thinking because-

a. Any level of defects is unacceptable.
b. Statistical process control charts will always prove an AQL has not been achieved.
c. An AQL establishes a level of non-conformance when the goal should be zero defects.
d. AQL is a measurement of personal performance, and contemporary theory holds that management is 85 percent responsible for quality.

3. The Purpose of attribute sampling is to -

a. Determine whether a batch conforms to the specifications
b. Make sure that every item is tested individually
c. Check on the quality of the inspection process
d. Identify which employees are producing defective items

4. What is the mean, median & mode of the following numbers; 2 6 10 12 12 18

a. 12,6, 10
b. 6,11,12
c. 10,11,12
d. 10,12,11

5. Kaisen is an approach to continuous improvement that emphasises-

a. Incremental improvement
b. The use of quality circles
c. Zero defects
d. Customer satisfaction over cost

6. Which of the following is not a Six Sigma concept?

a. DMAIC
b. DMAIM
c. DMADV
d. DFSS

7. An organisation whose project management process is certified as ISO 9000 has submitted a proposal to your firm along with a copy of the certification. This certificate indicates that-

a. The proposed project manager meets certain minimum qualifications as established by the standard
b. The products produced by the seller have met general industry-wide standards of quality
c. The process used by the seller to produce products or deliver services is documented, adhered to, and effective
d. The seller has demonstrated success on previous projects and is citing its past performance as an indicator of future performance

8. The 80/20 rule, also known as the Pareto Principle, is best described by which one of the following statements:

a. 80% of the problems in quality can be ascribed to management and 20% to the employees.
b. 80% of the cost of a product or service is in 20 % of the materials or labour required.
c. 80% of the time associated with a project is in 20 % of the tasks.
d. 80% percent of all problems are due to 20 % of all the types of problems that occur.

9. Conventional wisdom (pre Crosby, Juran, Deming, et al.) regarding quality performance standards says that error is-

a. Inevitable
b. Beneficial because we all learn from our mistakes
c. More the result of management than the person performing the job
d. Unlikely if there are sufficient inspectors in the process

10. The operative principle of quality function deployment (QFD) is that_

a. Employees are empowered and deployed to perform in conformance with the requirements, even if it means a decrease in production
b. A separate organisation known as QFD is responsible for quality throughout the organisation
c. Product design should always be chosen based on the needs of the ultimate customer or user
d. The level of quality of a product or service is a balance between the function the customer requires and the cost to deliver that function

11. Quality management includes the processes required to ensure that the project will satisfy-

a. Specifications developed by the technical staff
b. Legal requirements of the contract
c. Expectations of all stakeholders
d. Needs for which it was undertaken

12. The three components of quality management are-

a. Inspections, certifications, and validations
b. Planning, assurance, and control
c. Form, fit, and function
d. Reliability, maintainability, and availability

13. The temporary nature of a project means that investments in product quality improvement, especially defect prevention and appraisal, must often be borne by the-

a. Project manager
b. Performing organisation
c. Stakeholders
d. Customer

14. Quality Assurance is defined as-

a. A structured approach used to verify that a set of required steps has been performed
b. A process where measuring, examining, and testing are used to determine if quality has been achieved
c. A one-time activity used to establish project quality standards
d. All activities to provide confidence that the project will satisfy the relevant quality standards

15. The advantage of statistical sampling is best described by which of the following statements:

a. Does not require an expenditure of resources
b. Is accurate enough with a sampling of less than 1 percent
c. Does not require 100% inspection of the elements to achieve a satisfactory inference of the population
d. Needs to be conducted only when there is a problem discovered with the end product or the customer rejects

16 . Crosby's 4 absolutes of quality are?

a. Conformance to requirements/Prevention/Zero Defects/Measurement of Quality
b. Conformance to requirements/Prevention/Zero Defects/Compliance
c. Quality Management/Quality Planning/Quality Assurance/Quality Control
d. Plan/Do/Check/Act

17. With regard to the traditional project triangle of cost, schedule, and quality Where is Quality ranked?

a. First as the prime driver for a project
b. Second behind cost, but ahead of schedule
c. Second behind schedule, but ahead of cost
d. It depends on the nature of the project

18. In dealing with customers' complaints, it is important to-

a. Never deliver beyond the terms of the warranty
b. Talk to them until they see the reason the complaints are trivial
c. Give them something more than they contracted to receive to suppress any feelings of dissatisfaction
d. Provide them with the full scope of the contracted product or service

19. A cause and effect diagram is also called a-

a. Pareto chart
b. Statistical process control chart
c. Fishbone diagram
d. Design of experiments report

20. Quality is one part of the three major parameters of a project. When the quality in a project exceeds the specifications, it is called-

a. Excellence
b. Superior quality
c. Delighting the customer
d. Gold plating

21. The purpose of flowcharting is to—

a. Help analyse how problems occur
b. Show dependencies between tasks
c. Show the results of a process
d. Forecast future outcomes

22. In quality planning, the quality policy should be set by the—

a. Head of the organization
b. Project manager
c. Project team
d. Functional managers

23. All the following are aspects of 6 sigma except..

a. Aim is zero defects
b. Uses Black Belts
c. First time yield
d. Rule of 7

24. The best way to reduce the cost of quality control is to—

a. Make sure that the overall quality program is ISO compliant
b. Use statistical sampling techniques
c. Reduce the frequency of testing
d. Have more regular inspections

25. The continuous improvement process provides a way for an organization to create and sustain a culture of continuous improvement. As such, it should be directed by—

a. The project manager
b. Top management
c. Employees participating in quality circles
d. Stakeholders

26. Design of Experiments is a generic technique for--

a. Comparing the efficiency of different quality strategies
b. Identifying which variables are contributing to a given effect
c. Improving production processes
d. Making research projects more efficient

27. The Plan, Do, Check, Act cycle is associated with--

a. Deming
b. Crosby
c. Juran
d. Taguchi

28. A component has a specification of 12 cm with a permitted tolerance of .015 cm and the process that produces it has an inherent standard deviation of .002 cm. Which of the following is true?

a. The Process Capability Index is 2.5
b. This is an example of "Gold Plating"
c. The Voice of the Process exceeds the Voice of the Customer
d. All are true

29. The Kanban technique is an approach that supports the

a. Taguchi method
b. Just-in-time concept
c. Development of Pareto diagrams
d. Development of Ishikawa or fishbone diagrams

30. The ISO9000 standards provide..

a. A description of how products should be produced
b. Specifics for the implementation of quality systems
c. A framework around which an organisation can build a quality system
d. The maximum process requirements necessary to ensure that customers receive a good product

31. To effectively use statistical quality control, the project team should know the differences between—

a. Prevention and quality control
b. Assignable causes and random causes
c. Attribute sampling and statistical sampling
d. Control limits and operational definitions

32. Quality control should be performed—

a. When the product of the project is complete to ensure that no defects exist
b. Throughout the project
c. During the closeout phase but before final acceptance by the customer
d. As desired by the quality assurance department

33. A Pareto diagram is used to—

a. Show how many results were generated, by type or category of identified cause
b. Forecast future outcomes based on historical results
c. Show which variables have the most influence on the overall outcome
d. Show how various causes and sub-causes combine to create potential problems or effects

34. Which of the following defines the Juran Trilogy?

a. Quality Planning, Quality Control, Quality Assurance
b. Quality Planning, Quality Control, Quality Management
c. Quality Planning, Quality Control, Quality Improvement
d. None of the above

35. The statistical control chart is a tool used primarily to help—

a. Monitor process variation over time
b. Measure the degree of conformance
c. Determine whether results conform
d. Determine whether results conform to requirements

36. The quality management plan describes all the following *except* the

a. Method for implementing the quality policy
b. Project quality system
c. Organizational structure, responsibilities, procedures, processes, and resources needed to implement project quality management
d. Procedures used to conduct trade-off analyses among cost, schedule, and quality

PRACTICE QUESTION ANSWERS

		Page	Paragraph	
1	B	120	5.4	
2	C	110	2.8	
3	A	112	4.3	
4	C	114	4.8	
5	A	121	6.1	
6	B	124	6.13	
7	C	123	6.11	
8	D	117	5.2	
9	A	110	2.8	
10	C	123	6.9	
11	D	108	2.2	This is another way of saying fitness for purpose
12	B	108	1	This answer aligns with the 3 major Quality Management processes
13	B	-	-	This should be self evident
14	D	108	1.2	
15	C	112	4.1	
16	A	109	2.6	
17	D	122	6.4	There will be instances where to meet budget or schedule constraints there may be a requirement to sacrifice quality.
18	D	108	2.1	You should deliver to contract but it is better to deliver slightly over than slightly under.
19	C	118	5.30	Also called an Ishikawa diagram after its inventor
20	D	108	2.1	
21	C	117	5.1	
22	A	111	3.2	Quality has to be driven from the top
23	D	123	6.13	Rule of 7 concerns control charts
24	B	112	4.2/3	
25	B	121	6.1	
26	B	124	6.14	
27	A	122	6.7	
28	D	121	5.5	
29	B	122	6.3	
30	C	123	6.11	
31	B	120	5.4	They should know them all but the best answer is b)
32	B	-	-	This should be self evident
33	C	117	5.20	
34	C	123	6.8	
35	A	118	5.4	
36	D	110	3.1	

Chapter 7

Project Human Resource Management

1 Project Human Resource Management Processes

Project Human Resource Management consists of all those processes required to make the most effective use of all of the personnel involved in the project. This includes all of the project stakeholders such as customers, partners, sponsors and team members. The processes are:-

1.1 Develop Human Resource Plan

This is concerned with identifying and documenting project roles and responsibilities and reporting relationships. As a minimum the plan should include the following.

- Defined roles and responsibilities for all team members
- Organisation chart
- Staff management plan showing how and when people are deployed
- Training plan
- Recognition & reward scheme
- Health, Safety and Regulations as appropriate to the project

A key tool in defining roles and responsibilities is the Responsibility Assignment Matrix or RAM. This is simply a matrix showing tasks against people.

This concept can be expanded to show other task responsibilities
e.g. R = Responsible; A = Authorise; S = Support; C = Consult; I = Inform.
This is known as a RASCI chart

1.2 Acquire Project Team

This process involves obtaining the people necessary for completion of the project. Some members will be pre-assigned and others may be obtained from within the organisation by negotiation or may be acquired externally.

It is the responsibility of the project manager to lead the process of acquiring the project team, both by direct action and by influencing and negotiating with those capable of providing the resources.

The availability of e-mail and video conferencing and company intranets make possible the use of virtual teams. Virtual teams can work anywhere as they have little or no face to face communication. However in such an environment it is difficult to develop a true team spirit.

1.3 Develop Project Team

This consists of those activities that are required to develop and improve the skills and competencies of the project team. This is developed in more detail later in this chapter.

1.4 Manage Project Team

This is about monitoring team member performance, motivating and leading the team and resolving issues. Once again this topic is covered in detail later in this chapter.

2 Organisational Theories

2.1 Functional Organisation

Used mainly where the project lies entirely or mainly within a single Function, or where a project passes from Function to Function e.g. product development. Often used for less important projects or in organisations with no project management culture. An example structure is shown below.

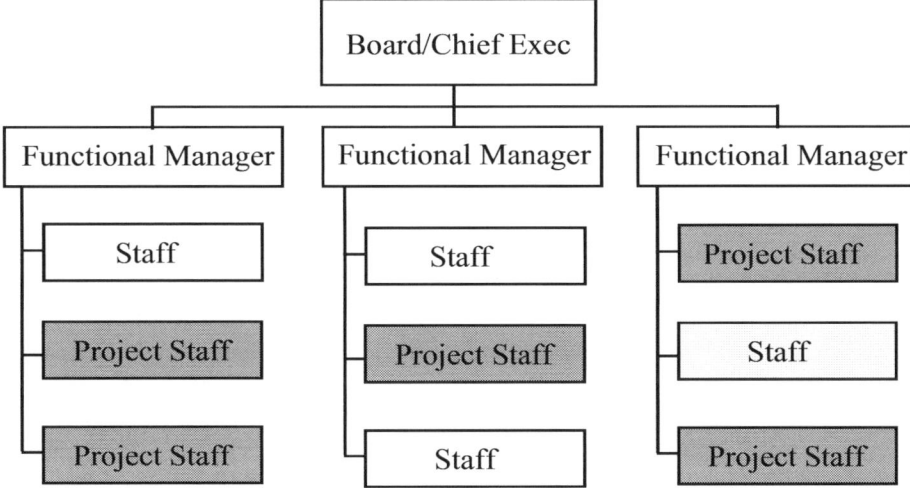

Functional structure

There may or may not be a named project manager/leader/coordinator within particular functions or covering the whole project. However such a person will have minimal power within their function and virtually none outside it. The Functional Managers coordinate all the activities and make all the major decisions.

2.2 Matrix Organisations

The matrix organisation shown overleaf maintains the vertical functional lines of authority while establishing a relatively permanent horizontal structure to support cross-functional projects. The project managers interact with all functional units that support their projects and provide resource. This structure also promotes more efficient use of scarce resources. The downside is that communications are more complex and there can be problems caused by conflicting priorities of Project and Functional managers.

Weak Matrix

A weak matrix structure is very similar to a functional structure except that responsibility for coordination has been delegated to project staff. There is often a named project manager/leader/coordinator but with limited authority, especially outside their own function. Power remains with the functional managers.

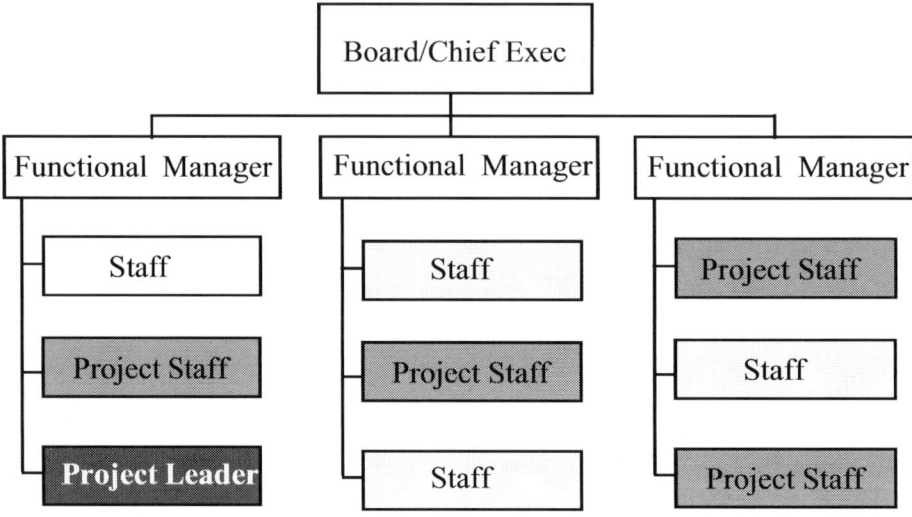

Weak Matrix Structure

Balanced Matrix

In a balanced matrix there is a named project manager with referent power from the functional manager and from the CEO. The project manager coordinates all project activities. Power is balanced between project and functional managers. The structure appears identical to a weak matrix

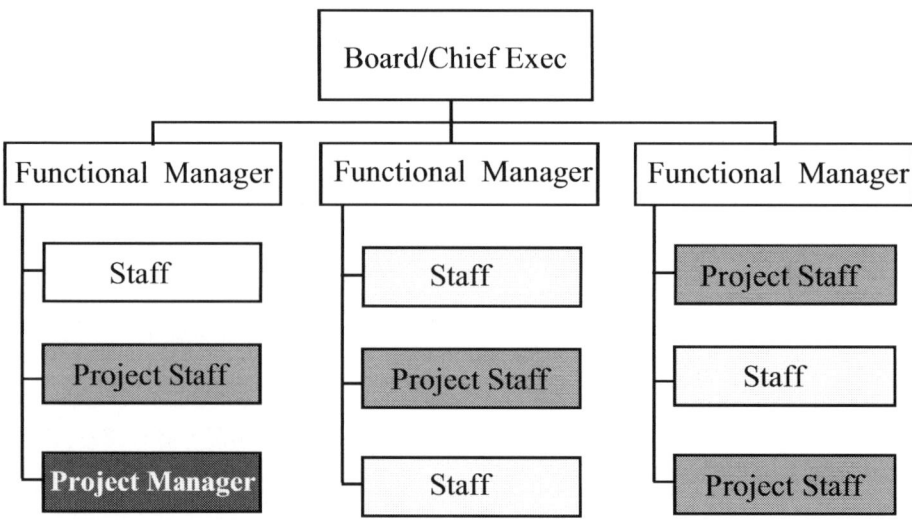

Balanced matrix structure

Strong Matrix

A strong matrix is a radical change from weak and balanced matrices. Project managers now operate from a separate function under their own management that reports directly to the CEO. The PM is now fully independent of the functional managers and once functional managers allocate staff to a project they are under the control of the project manager. As in the other matrix structures, the functional managers retain line management responsibility for their staff but their day to day project activities are controlled by the PM or his/her delegates

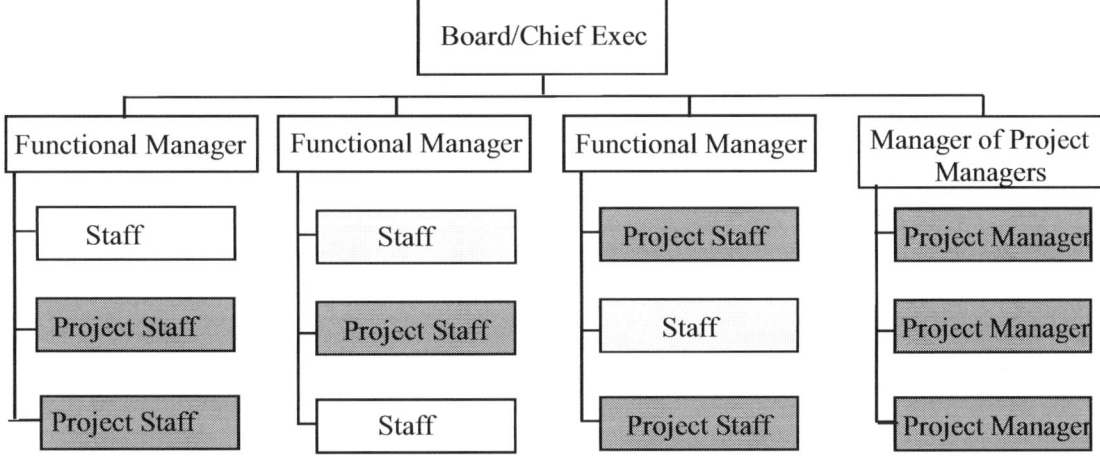

A strong matrix structure

2.3 Projectised Structure

There is a separate, vertical structure established for each individual project and the project manager has total authority over the project. Such project structures are typically used by organisations whose main business consists of large capital projects such as roads, bridges, tunnels and large buildings. In this situation the project manager has total control over all resources and reports directly to a senior executive.

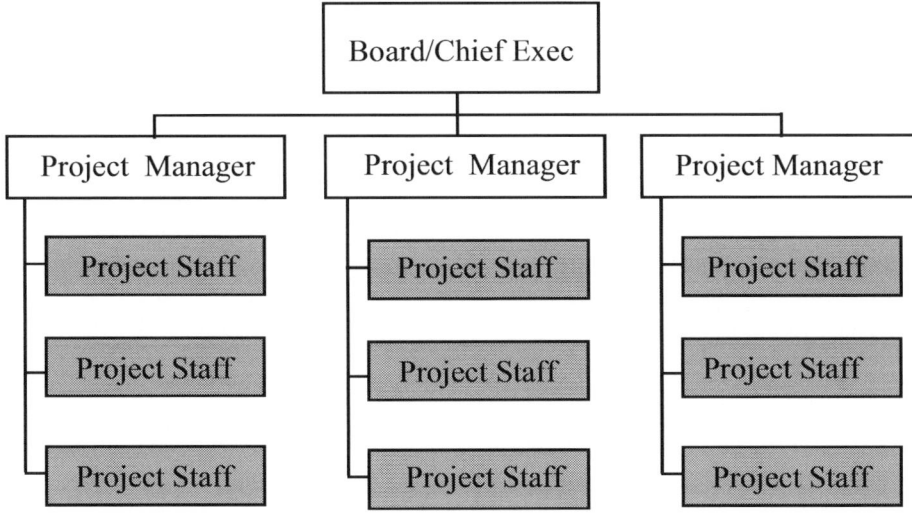

2.4 Composite Organisation

Not all structures fall into such neat groupings and many companies involve all the structures at various levels within the company. Such organisations are called Composite.

2.5 Project Manager Titles

There is no consistency amongst project management titles. Lower level project managers operating in functional or weak matrix situations are sometimes referred to as Project Expediters, Project Co-ordinators or Project Leaders. The Expediter role is often the more junior being little more than a message passer. More senior project managers are often referred to as Program Managers or Project/Program Directors.

3 Project Manager Roles and Responsibilities

3.1 Functions of the Project Manager

A Project Manager has four basic functions

1 **Planning**
Determining the time, cost and resources needed to complete the project.

2 **Organising**
Co-ordination of the mixture of human, financial and physical assets

3 **Leading**
Essential to combine the efforts of Planning and Organising.

4 **Controlling**
Monitor progress in relation to time, cost & quality/scope

3.2 Roles of the Project Manager

The project manager must fill many roles including-

Integrator: Important because the project manager is the only person able to view both the project and the way it fits the overall plan for the organisation.

Communicator: Important because the project manager who fails to decipher and pass on appropriate information on time can 'become the major bottleneck in a project.

Team Leader: The project manager must be able to solve problems as they arise, guide people from different functional areas, and co-ordinate the project to show leadership capabilities. Prior supervisory experience is required for all project managers.

Decision Maker: The project manager must be able to make decisions including the allocation of resources, the costs of performance and schedule trade-offs, and changing the scope, direction, or characteristics of the project.

Climate Creator/Builder: Project manager should attempt to build a supportive atmosphere so that the project team members can work together and not against each other. In particular, in a matrix environment, the PM must overcome the problems of split loyalty of team members between the Project and their owning Function.

4 Team Building

Team building is the responsibility of the Project Manager and should be a concerted effort at the start of every new project

4.1 Why Team Building?

Total team effort is required-the team is much more than the sum of its parts.

The project manager has unique responsibilities because:-

- The team consists of a diverse collection of individuals with widely differing backgrounds, abilities, needs, and interests

- Team members are unfamiliar with project goals and individuals' capabilities are unknown to the project manager

- Matrix management mode makes it hard to obtain real commitments from team members who may work on the project part-time

Team building should become very high on a project manager's priority list.

4.2 The Need for Team Building

How do you know that your project needs team building? To make this determination, look for some of the following symptoms, which indicate that bad teamwork exists:

Frustration: Characterised by negative attitudes, grumbling, and poor productivity

Conflict and unhealthy competition: Characterised by intense rivalry or even constant war between individuals or groups. Bickering, "backbiting," and "dirty tricks" are common events.

Unproductive meetings: Meetings that turn into "gripe sessions " where management does all the talking, or where the project manager "lays down the law."

Lack of trust in the project manager: A project manager who has become isolated from the team members will be very ineffective.

4.3 The Team Building Process

The following diagram shows activities taking place that facilitate progress through the cycle.

This is the Tuckman **Forming/Storming/Norming/Performing** model of team development.

This is a well recognised process that all teams go through. The job of the PM is to get the team performing and keep them there.

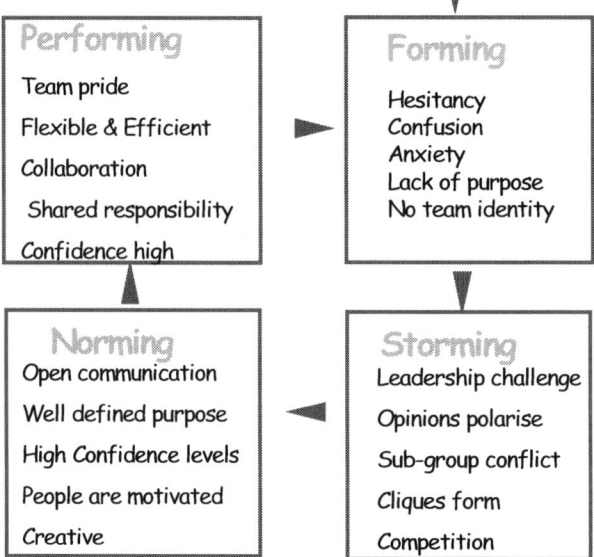

Some authorities add a fifth stage called **Adjourning** that is associated with project closure.

The following shows the project activities normally required to progress from one stage to the next.

Forming to Storming>   Occurs during Concept/Initiation.

Typical activities:- Business Planning ,Milestone Planning, Organisation Planning

Storming to Norming>   Associated with Detailed Planning stage

Typical activites:- WBS, Schedule construction, Risk planning, Resource Planning

Norming to Performing>   Associated with Execution Phase

Typical activities:- Cost Control, Schedule Control, Risk Management, Change Control

Performing to Norming/Storming> This is regressive behaviour

Typical causes:- Major changes, severe project problems, staff changes, poor leadership

4.4 Goals/Results of Project Team Building

- A readiness to work towards a common good
- Loyalty to other team workers
- Identification with the team
- A willingness to maximise personal effort for the team good.
- Sacrifice of personal interest for the good of the whole

A well-functioning team can often produce results that far exceed the potential output of its individual members. The terms synergism and symbiosis have been used to describe this effect (i.e., 2 + 2 = 5).

4.5 Ground Rules for Project Team Building

- Start the project of with a "kick off" meeting of all the team members
- Continue team building through the life of the project
- Recruit the best possible people
- Make sure that everyone who will significantly contribute to the project is on the team
- Obtain team agreement on all major actions
- Recognise the existence of team politics but stay out of them
- Behave as a role model
- Use delegation as the best way to assure commitment
- Don't try to force or manipulate team members
- Regularly evaluate team effectiveness
- Plan and use a team-building process
- Put in place an effective reward & recognition system.

4.6 War Room & Tight Matrix

A War Room is a dedicated room allocated to the project team where they can all work together in a single location. Teamwork and Communications are enhanced when a team works in close proximity to each other. Such an arrangement is known as a Tight Matrix. Do not confuse this with matrix management. The *PMBOK® Guide* also uses the term Co-location to describe having the project team in one location. If co-location is not possible it is even more important to gain the co-operation of the resident functional managers.

5 Types of Power

A Project Manager can exert the following types of power:

5.1 Legitimate Power

Legitimate power is power that the project manager has because of his/her position within the organisation. Successful use of this power is generally in conjunction with expert and reward power.

5.2 Penalty or Coercive Power

Penalty power is based on the fear of a subordinate that something bad may happen to him for failing to do what the project manager asks. This is a subset of Legitimate Power.

5.3 Reward Power

Reward power is the opposite of Penalty power. It involves the ability to reward people in exchange for positive achievements. Once again this is a form of Legitimate Power.

5.4 Expert Power

Expert power is exercised by project managers who are respected because of reputation based on their knowledge, skill and experience.

5.5 Referent Power

Referent power is based being seen to have the backing of a more powerful person as the basis for one's own authority.

PMI recommends that project managers rely on reward and expert power to the greatest extent possible, and that they avoid use of coercive power.

6 Project Conflict

Project Managers must recognise that conflict in projects is unavoidable and needs to be actively managed. Conflict is natural and can be beneficial as lack of conflict can signify apathy. Conflicts must be resolved to the benefit of the project, concentrating on the issue and not the personalities.

6.1 Sources of Conflict

Research has demonstrated there are there are seven principal sources of conflict on a typical project ordered as follows.

1. Conflict over project priorities.

Project team disagree over sequencing of activities and tasks

2. Conflict over Admin procedures.

Differences over how the project will be organised and administered

3. Conflict over technical opinions and performance trade offs.

4. Conflict over Manpower

Conflicts concerning resourcing of staff from other areas

5. Conflict over Cost

Arguments with support areas over cost of project elements

6. Conflict over Schedules

Disagreements over timing and scheduling of tasks and activities

7. Personality Conflicts

6.2 Conflict by Phase

The highest-ranked sources of conflict evident in each phase of the project life cycle are-

- **Concept Phase**: Project priorities, administrative procedures, and schedules
- **Planning Phase**: Project priorities, schedules, and administrative procedures
- **Implementation Phase**: Schedules, technical issues, and resources
- **Project close-out Phase**: Schedules, personality conflicts, and resources

6.3 Conflict Management

The effect of conflict on a project depends primarily on how it is handled. There are many ways of handling conflict. PMI define the following methods.

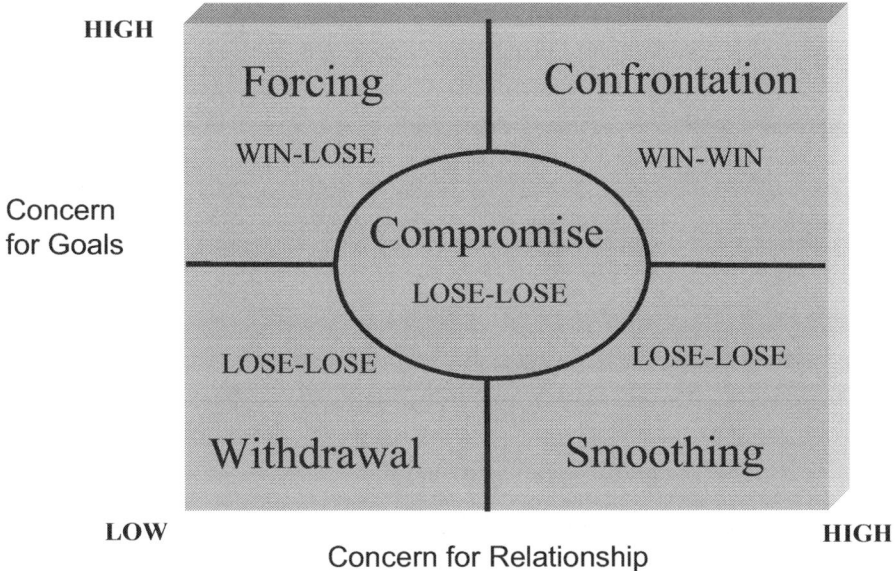

1. Withdrawing/Avoiding

This is the do nothing option. Just ignore the problem. This shows low concern for both the problem and the ongoing relationship and is a lose-lose situation as the conflict still exists.

2. Smoothing/Accommodating

In this situation the parties wish to remain friends and therefore try and smooth over their disagreement perhaps by emphasizing areas of agreement or by one party accommodating the views of the other. This is still lose-lose as the underlying conflict still exists and the problem has not been solved

3. Compromising

A middle way is found that both parties can accept. Relationships are protected but this is still lose-lose because neither party gets everything they want and must give something up.

4. Forcing

In this situation one party to the conflict has authority over the other and has imposed their preferred solution. From the point of view of the winner the problem has been solved, but at the expense of the relationship. This is a win-lose situation.

5. Confrontation/Problem Solving

In this scenario both parties together explore the best solution to the problem i.e. they confront the issue, not each other. During this process one or both parties may change their view but they both agree that the resulting solution is the best and because of this and the fact that the relationship has been maintained, or even enhanced, this is win-win.

PMI refer to a sixth technique called **Collaborating** but this is essentially a form of **Confrontation/ Problem Solving** as it involves cooperating to obtain the best solution.

7 Leadership Styles

The four leadership extremes

1. Autocratic:

Managers solicit little or no information input from their group and make the decisions solely by themselves

2. Consultative autocrat:

Managers solicit input but make the decisions solely by themselves.

3. Consensus manager:

Throws open the problem to the group for discussion and simultaneously allows or encourages the entire group to make the relevant decision. This style is also called **Democratic.**

4. Laissez-Faire:

This position is literally poor management. The manager has minimal communication with the group and delegate authority to it to make decisions. It is virtually abdication of management.

The method of leading which gives the most lasting result is Consultive Autocratic. However leaders must be flexible in their approach. Although the Consultive Autocratic approach is the best long term strategy there may be instances where in the short term another method may be more appropriate.

8 Motivation Theories

Four theories need to be understood:

1. Maslow's hierarchy of needs

2. McGregor's theory X and theory Y

3. Herzberg's theory of motivation

4. Expectancy theory.

8.1 Maslow's Hierarchy of Needs

Maslow's theory is based on a hierarchy of 5 needs. One cannot proceed to the next level until the previous level is fulfilled.

- **Physiological needs**; Air, Water, Food, Clothing

- **Safety**: The need for security and safety-from danger, threat, and deprivation

- **Relationships**: The need for association with others for love, affection, friendship and approval

- **Esteem**: The need for self-respect and the respect and approval of one's fellows.

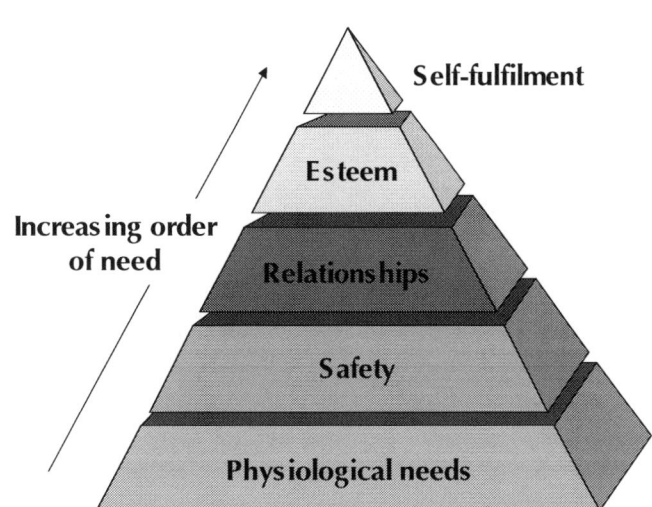

- **Self-fulfilment**: The need to
grow and learn and have the opportunity to be creative. This is also known as **self-actualisation.**

This is a generalised model and the table on the next page shows how this relates to the working environment and organisational factors.

Needs level	General Rewards	Organisational factors
1 Physiological	Food, water, sleep	Pay Pleasant working conditions Cafeteria
2 Safety	Safety, security, stability, protection	Safe working conditions Company benefits Job security
3 Social	Friendship, affection, belongingness	Cohesive work group Friendly supervision Professional associations
4 Esteem	Self-esteem, self-respect, prestige, status	Social recognition Job title High status job
5 Self-actualisation	Growth, advancement, creativity	Challenging job Opportunities for creativity Achievement in work Advancement

8.2 McGregor's Theory X and Theory Y

McGregor claimed that most workers fell into shades of two basic categories.

Theory X   The average worker is:-

- Inherently lazy and avoids work whenever possible
- Must be supervised and directed
- Needs the threat of punishment to work
- Avoids responsibility

Management until fairly recent times was based on this theory. It relies on external motivation such as strict rules, performance incentives and threats to job security.

Theory Y   In this theory:-

- People are not by nature resistant to organisational needs.
- They are willing and eager to accept responsibility
- They do not require constant supervision
- They seek opportunity for personal improvement and self respect

Management can take advantage of this scenario by creating an environment where workers own goals coincide with organisational objectives.

8.3 Herzberg's Theory of Motivation

Herzberg developed a theory of motivation based on what he describes as Hygiene Factors and Motivators.

Examples of Hygiene Factors

- Working conditions
- Salary
- Quality of management/supervision

Satisfactory hygiene factors are necessary, but not sufficient for a contented worker. Poor hygiene factors may destroy motivation; but improving hygiene factors under normal circumstances is not likely to increase motivation.

Examples of Motivators

- Recognition
- Work content
- Responsibility
- Growth

Positive motivation results from an opportunity to achieve and experience self-actualisation. The worker should have a sense of personal growth and responsibility. The absence of Motivators, even when Hygiene factors are present will lead to reduction in job performance.
The theory does not always hold true. There are many cases where strong motivators can overcome poor hygiene factors.

8.4 Expectancy Theory

This is a simple theory that states that people will tend to be highly productive and motivated if two conditions are satisfied:

1. They believe that their efforts will lead to successful results

2. They will be rewarded for their contribution to that success.

If their expectations are not met then they will be demotivated.

9 Management by Objectives

MBO is a system of managerial leadership that defines individual managerial responsibilities in terms of corporate objectives. Managers are set individual goals that contribute to the achievement of those corporate objectives. MBO really only works well when it is driven by top management. For a project manager, the goals and objectives should reflect the goals of the project and should also align well with the customer's or client's goals.

MBO is a three-step process:

1. Establish unambiguous and realistic objectives

   - Good objectives are unambiguously stated and contain a measure of how to assess whether they have been achieved.

   - To be realistic, objectives must be determined jointly by managers and those who are to perform the work-a top-down, bottom-up process.

2. Periodically evaluate whether project objectives are being achieved

3. Act upon the results of the evaluation

The WBS aligns well with MBO because the delivery of individual work packages or groups of work packages can establish measurable objectives.

10 The Halo Effect

In Performance Appraisal the Halo Effect is where there is a tendency for a high or low appraisal score on one performance objective to influence the appraiser on other objectives.

Human Resource Management Practice Questions

1. The most common areas of conflict are—

a. Project office, functional divisions, field sites, and corporate offices
b. Project priorities, personnel resources, technical issues, scheduling issues
c. Team building, team integration, functional co-ordination, customer expectations
d. Team members, subcontractor management, stakeholder management, client co-ordination

2. All the following assumptions about employees are held by Theory X managers and except—

a. Most people think work is distasteful and try to avoid it
b. Most people prefer to be directed and must often be forced to do their work
c. Most people are not ambitious, do not want get ahead, and do not want responsibility
d. Most people are motivated primarily by their desire for self-fulfilment (self actualisation)

3. Herzberg's theory of motivation holds that if motivators such as achievement, recognition and responsibility are not present, employees will—

a. Become disillusioned and look for other employment
b. Lack motivation but still work well
c. Lack motivation and become dissatisfied with their work
d. Use the workplace as a means to extend their social life

4. There can be problems when using MBO in a project environment because--

a. MBO has not been a great success in normal operational environments so it will probably fail in a project environment.
b. MBO implies that employees jointly establish their own goals. In a project environment the goals are dictated by the project.
c. Managers dislike the MBO approach, because they believe project managers will establish goals that can be achieved with relative ease.
d. Most projects fail to meet their objectives for reasons outside the scope of the team so establishing objectives using MBO is unfair.

5. "Pay attention everyone, just calm down, stop arguing and get on with the job" is an example of which type of conflict management strategy?

a. Smoothing
b. Confrontation
c. Avoidance
d. Compromise

6. The project expediter has the greatest level of authority-

a. Across all functions
b. Within the function headed by his own manager
c. On technical issues
d. In acquiring material resources

7. The condition where employees are primarily motivated by the desire for personal growth is called-

a. Expectancy
b. Theory Y
c. Hygiene factor
d. Self-actualisation

8. Good project managers mainly use the following sources of power.

a. Reward and Expert
b. Reward and Legitimate
c. Legitimate and Expert
d. Reward and Coercive

9. Which of the following leadership styles in the long run gives best results?

a. Consensus
b. Democratic
c. Laissez-Faire
d. Consultative autocratic

10. Being influenced in an assessment by previous good performance is an example of?

a. Maslow's theory
b. Management by objectives
c. The Halo effect
d. Expectancy Theory

11. In a projectised structure, the project manager typically-

a. Reports directly to the Board of Directors or CEO
b. Directly controls all human resources
c. Needs strong technical skills
d. Operates primarily through a deputy project manager

12. In a weak matrix-

a. Nobody is in charge
b. Projects are not thought to be as important as operations
c. The balance of power is shifted toward the functional manager
d. Projects are usually minor and of short duration

13. Which of the following conflict management approaches is usually least effective?

a. Smoothing
b. Problem-solving
c. Confrontation
d. Compromise

14. Adjusting when non critical tasks occur, without delaying the project is known as—

a. Resource levelling
b. Resource smoothing
c. Resource management
d. Resource adjustment

15. The best way to create project identity and foster ongoing teamwork is to—

a. Organise a project team "away day"
b. Establish a "war room"
c. Establish clear lines of authority
d. Encourage initiative

16. A key component of concurrent engineering is-

a. Placing all work under the control of a single function
b. Creating teams that have representatives from different project phases
c. Involving the implementers of a project in the design phase
d. To make maximum use of a strong matrix

17. Output per person per hour of input describes-

a. Economies of scale
b. Value marginal product (MVP)
c. Productivity
d. The learning curve

18. Which project structure is most likely to generate conflict between the PM and functional managers

a. Weak Matrix
b. Balanced Matrix
c. Strong Matrix
d. Projectised Structure

19. Which of the following resolution approaches is likely to lead to the most lasting solutions?

a. Forcing
b. Smoothing
c. Compromise
d. Confrontation

20. In a strong matrix environment, the functional manager's major responsibilities include-

a. Deciding what is to be done
b. Signing off the project plan
c. Approving the budget
d. Providing resources to do the work

21. Which of the following is associated with detailed planning?

a. Forming to Storming
b. Storming to Norming
c. Norming to Performing
d. Storming to Performing

22. A constraining factor that may affect the organization of the project team is—

a. The organizational structure of the performing organization
b. Poor communication among team members
c. Ambiguous staffing requirements
d. Team morale

23. A project is managed by a project coordinator or leader. Which kind of organisation is it most likely to be?

a. A weak matrix.
b. A balanced matrix
c. A strong matrix.
d. A projectised organisation

24. Team members are often accountable to both a functional manager and the project manager. Who has the prime responsibility for managing this situation?

a. Team members involved
b. Project manager
c. Project owner or sponsor
d. Functional manager

25. Which of the following is not considered by Hertzberg to be a motivating factor?

a. Increased responsibility
b. Salary increase
c. Recognition
d. Job satisfaction

26. All the following have been found to be major barriers to building effective project teams except

a. Differing priorities, interests, and judgments of team members
b. Role conflicts
c. Lack of team member commitment
d. Amount of office space allocated to each member

27. Your newly formed project team do not all know each other and you do not know all of them. How would you best ensure a successful start up?

a. Produce a document assigning roles and responsibilities
b. Distribute the project plan
c. Organise a kick off meeting
d. Individually meet with each project team member

28. Which of the following is generally not regarded to be a motivator according to Herzberg?

a. Working conditions and interpersonal relations
b. Responsibility for enlarged task.
c. Interest in the task
d. Recognition for achievement

29. A manager who makes decisions without considering the information provided by project team members is using which management style?

a. Laissez-faire
b. Autocratic
c. Bureaucratic
d. Judicious

30. A project's reward and recognition system should—

a. Include training as one of its elements
b. Discourage undesired behaviour and encourage desired behaviour
c. Be the same as that of the performing organization
d. Make the link between performance and reward clear, explicit, and achievable

31. Which statement is true regarding conflict in projects?

a. A matrix form of organization can produce a lack of clear role definitions and lead to ambiguous jurisdictions between and among functional leaders and project managers.
b. Sources of conflict include project priorities, PERT/CPM schedules, contract administrative procedures, and type of contract.
c. Conflict is to be avoided whenever possible.
d. Strong matrix project managers have few human resource conflicts, because they can dictate their needs to functional managers.

32. The terms strong matrix and weak matrix when applied to project organizations have implications for--

a. The ability of the organization to achieve its goals
b. The physical proximity of project team members to one another and to the project manager
c. The degree of authority the project manager has over team resources
d. The degree to which team members bond together

33. The chances for successful completion of a multidisciplinary project are increased if project team members are

a. Problem oriented
b. Politically sensitive to top management's needs
c. Focused on individual project activities
d. Focused on customer demands

34. Team performance is based on the

a. Organizational structure of the project
b. Training provided to the project team
c. Individual development of each team member
d. Project's climate of collaboration, pride and shared responsibility

35. The key way for a project manager to promote optimum team performance in project teams whose members are not co-located is to—

a. Build trust
b. Establish a reward and recognition system
c. Obtain the support of the functional managers in the other locations
d. Exercise his or her right to control all aspects of the project

36. Which of the following is a ground rule for project team building?

a. Do frequent performance reviews
b. Ensure that each team member still reports to his/her functional manager
c. Start the process as soon as possible with a kick off meeting
d. Get involved to sort out personality clashes

PRACTICE QUESTION ANSWERS

		Page	Paragraph	
1	B	143	6.2	
2	D	146	8.2	
3	C	147	8.3	
4	B	147	9.0	
5	A	143	6.3	
6	B	135	2.2	
7	D	145	8.10	Self-actualisation is an alternative way of saying self-fulfilment
8	A	142	5.5	
9	D	144	7.0	
10	C	148	10.0	
11	A	138	2.5	
12	C	135	2.2	
13	A	143	6.3	
14	B	66	3.11	
15	B	141	4.6	
16	C	124	6.5	
17	C			Self evident
18	B	136	2.2	In a balanced matrix there is no clear statement of authority thus there is potential for conflict especially with managers of other functions.
19	D	144	6.3	Confrontation means jointly confronting the problem (not each other) to find a solution which both agree is the best.
20	D	135	2.2	
21	B	140	4.3	
22	A			Self evident
23	A	135	2.2	
24	B	138	3.2	
25	B	147	8.3	
26	A			Differing priorities, interests and judgements are to be expected in any team and should not be the cause of major conflicts.
27	C	141	4.5	
28	A	147	8.3	
29	B	144	7.1	
30	D	147	8.4	This is an example of Expectancy Theory
31	A	135	2.2	
32	C	135/7	2.2	
33	C			Self evident
34	D	140	4.3	
35	C	141	4.6	
36	C	141	4.5	

Chapter 8

Project Communications Management

1 Project Communications Management

Project Communications Management consists of those processes necessary to ensure the timely and appropriate treatment of all project information including generation, collection, dissemination and storage. The 5 major processes are summarized below.

1. Identify Stakeholders

Determining all interested and/or affected people and organisations

2. Plan Communications

Planning how to satisfy the information needs of the project stakeholders

3. Distribute Information

The various means of making appropriate information available to stakeholders in a timely manner

4. Manage Stakeholder Expectations

Actively managing communications and issues with stakeholders.

5. Performance Reporting

The provision of information on project status and forecasting the project outcome

1.1 Communication Dimensions

The ability to communicate effectively is a general management skill and has a number of dimensions:

- Internal (to the project) and External
- Formal and Informal
- Vertical (with seniors and subordinates) and horizontal (with peers and suppliers)
- Official and Unofficial
- Written and Spoken
- Face to face and Distant

1.2 Communication Skills

Effective communications is not a single skill but covers many different areas. A particularly important skill is to be a good listener. Listening skills include:-

- Being able to read body language and facial expressions
- Provide feedback to the listener to confirm understanding
- Not interrupting or talking over the speaker
- Taking notes

Other desirable skills are:-
- Be able to resolve conflicts
- Have powers of persuasion
- Be a good negotiator
- Be able to teach, train and impart knowledge
- Be able to gather facts and formulate an argument
- Be able to formulate and communicate a plan of action

1.3 The Communications Model

Communication skills are based on an understanding of the simple four element Communications Model. i.e.

a) **Communicator or Source:** – The person with whom the message originates.

b) **Message**:- The physical thought, idea, etc sent to the Receiver from the Source in a Code understood by both.

c) **Medium or Channel**:- The vehicle or method used to convey the message.

d) **Recipient**:- The recipient of the message. No communication has taken place until the receiver accepts and understands the message.

1.4 Filtering

Filtering occurs when a large proportion of a message is lost when passing from sender to receiver. Possible causes of filtering are:-

- Language; the same words can mean different things to different people.

- Culture; different ways of doing business.

- Knowledge base; different knowledge base may lead to misunderstanding

- Assumptions; the message may be based on incorrect assumptions

Messages are more likely to be understood correctly when there is active listening and feedback

1.5 Barriers to Communication

There are many barriers that can inhibit effective project communications: e.g.

- Lack of clear communications channels

- Differing individual perceptions

- Physical distance between the communicator and receiver

- Difficulties with technical language

- Hidden agendas

- Environmental distractions

- Hostile or disbelieving attitude

Note that the presence of communication barriers may lead to increased conflict!

2 Stakeholder Management

A Stakeholder is any person or body that is affected by your project or has an interest in it. The attitude and actions of Stakeholders can have a significant effect on the performance and outcome of your project and hence they must be managed. This is primarily the responsibility of the project manager, although for very senior stakeholders he may make use of the project sponsor.

The key way to manage stakeholders is via communication but this should be a planned proactive process and not just a reaction to issues.

2.1 The Stakeholder Management Process.

This process follows the same form as that for managing Risk i.e.

1. **Identification**
   Who are the project stakeholders, both supporters and opponents?
2. **Analysis**
   What is the position, power and influence of each individual stakeholder or stakeholder group?
3. **Formulate Action Plan**
   How do we proactively manage the stakeholders so as to benefit the project?
4. **Monitor and Control**
   Carry out and maintain the action plans

2.2 Stakeholder Identification

The most usual method of identification is by *Brainstorming*.
Potential stakeholders may include:

- Statutory and regulatory bodies
- The Performing Organisation

- The project team
- The Client/Sponsor
- Suppliers and Contractors
- End users
- People affected by the project
- People on the sidelines who may have strong feelings about the project; both positive and negative.

Relationships between stakeholders can be represented by a Stakeholder Map such as the example shown opposite which relates to an IT project in a manufacturing environment.

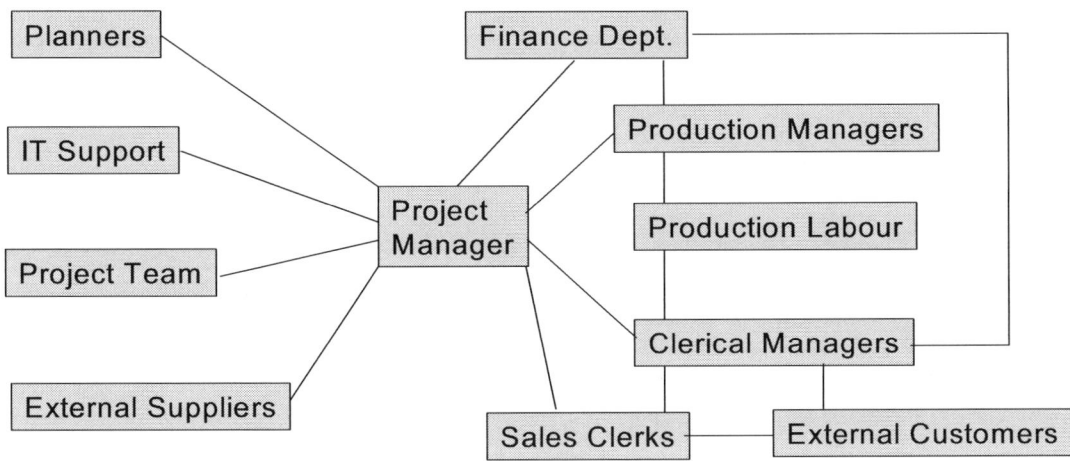

Details of identified stakeholders are captured in the Stakeholder Register that also tracks their status

2.3 Stakeholder Analysis

In the analysis stage it is necessary to try and discover the position of stakeholders with respect to the project. Consideration might be given to questions such as the following:

- Will they benefit from the success of the project?

- Will they be openly supportive of the project?

- Do they have reasons for wanting the project to fail?

- If their views are negative or ambivalent can they be persuaded to change?

- What is their level of power and influence?

There are several simple models that we can use to facilitate the analysis process. The *PMBOK® Guide* describes the Power/Interest grid shown below.

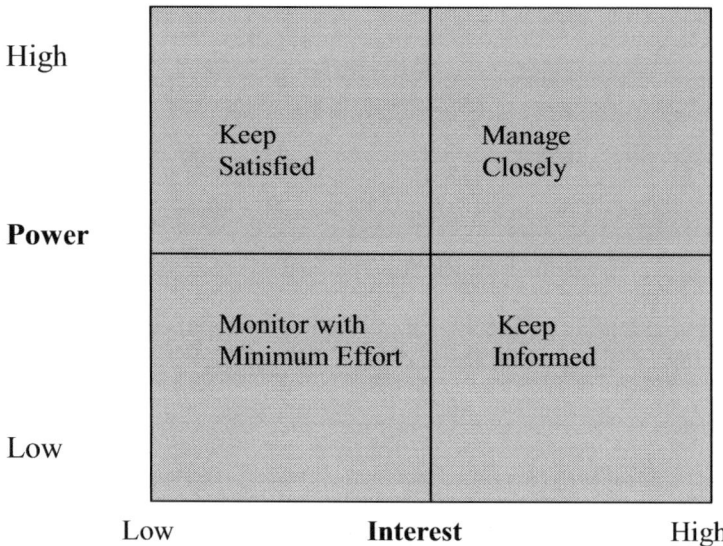

The weakness of this model is that it does not differentiate between +ve and –ve stakeholders. This is overcome by the superior, Power/Influence model shown below.

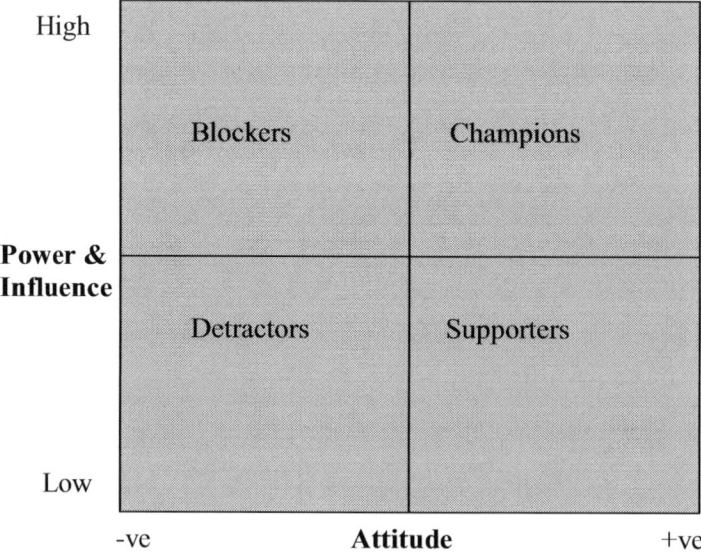

- **Champions** are powerful people who are actively supportive of the project.
- **Blockers** are powerful people who will actively resist the project.
- **Supporters** are people with little power who are in favour of the project.
- **Detractors** are people with little power who are against the project.

Bear in mind that Detractors and Supporters can organise themselves into focus groups and become Blockers and Champions respectively.

2.4 Stakeholder Action Plan

Planning consists of examining each stakeholder, trying to understand what motivates them and then formulating an action strategy to manage and influence them. A brief example based on the stakeholder map on the previous page is shown below.

Stakeholder	Attitude	Motivation	Actions
Production Manager	Champion	Success will increase productivity	Regular communication
Production Operatives	Blockers	Possible job losses	Negotiate severance pay and productivity bonus
Sales Clerks	Detractors	Think it will make their job harder	Involve in requirements and acceptance
IT Maintenance	Supporters	New system easier to maintain	Keep onside by regular updates & consultation

2.5 Managing Stakeholders

Stakeholders must be actively managed, especially as their views and motivation may change over the life of the project. The analysis must be repeated throughout the project lifecycle as new stakeholders appear and attitudes change. "Champions" can be used to managing or influencing "Blockers" or to organise "Supporters"

2.6 Issue Management

The management of stakeholders, although mainly a proactive process, will also involve the management of Issues. An Issue is a problem that requires immediate and/or ongoing attention. The document used to record and maintain status of issues is the Issue Log. Each issue must have an assigned owner and a target resolution date. Some issues arise from known risks. Others from unforeseen circumstances. Many companies maintain a combined Risk & Issues Log.

3 Remaining Communications Processes

3.1 Plan Communications
The output of "Plan Communications" is the Communications Management Plan It details the methods used to collect, store and disseminate information and to whom information flows. It is a sub-section of the project management plan.

Communications Management Plan Contents

- Stakeholder communication requirements

- Information to be communicated, including format, content, and level of detail

- Person responsible for communicating the information

- Person or groups who will receive the information

- Methods or technologies used to convey the information

- Frequency of the communication

- Escalation process

3.2 Distribute Information

This involves making information available in a timely fashion. It includes implementing the Communications Management Plan as well as responding to one off requests for information.

Elements of Information Distribution

- Project Records & Reports
- Presentations
- Stakeholder notifications and feedback
- Lessons Learned
- Change requests

3.3 Performance Reporting

Performance reporting is an important element of Communications Management. Its purpose is to keep stakeholders informed as to project progress, to explain causes of variation from the base line and to forecast project outcome.

A key element of performance reporting is reporting on and explaining reasons for deviations from the baseline plan, and then forecasting the expected effects on project cost, time and deliverables.

The *PMBOK® Guide* lists several forecasting methods. Of most relevance is Earned Value, which was discussed in Chapter 5.

Not all stakeholders require the same information so reports may need to be tailored for content and level of detail. In particular project financial information may be restricted.

Formal performance reporting should take place at regular set intervals. Monthly reporting is common but for relatively short projects and at times of critical activity then weekly reporting may be more appropriate. Most organisations will have a standard reporting format.

Although a formal performance report is a key document for shareholder communication it should not be used as the sole means of information distribution. Senior stakeholders should not first learn about major issues via a standard report. Always make them aware of major issues (and what you are doing about them) as soon as it is practical.

4 Building Effective Team Communications

Project managers spend about 90% of their time engaged in some form of communication. The project manager is responsible for building and maintaining communication links within the project team and with the outside world. Here are 4 areas of action to enhance project communications and team building.

1. Be an Effective Communicator

The project manager must recognise that effective communication is a 2 way process and that feedback is also bi-directional. He must communicate effectively by the most appropriate means.

2. Be a Communications Expediter

The project manager must bring people together and initiate relationships. He must develop communication channels and eliminate communication blockers whilst encouraging new ideas.

3. Make Meetings Effective

Meetings are essential for building teams, making group decisions, solving group problems, and achieving a group consensus. The project manager should adhere to the following guidelines for ensuring effective meetings that hold the attention and interest of all team members:

- Establish a meeting policy
- Only call a meeting when there is a real need
- Make the purpose of the meeting very clear
- Prepare an agenda
- Follow the agenda
- Encourage participation
- Include a team-building element
- Issue minutes
- Follow up on all task assignments and action items

Poor meetings are usually a result of poor preparation and an inept chairperson.

4. Eliminate Communications Blockers

Communications blockers are negative responses that kill or inhibit innovative ideas. For example:

- "It will never work."
-
- "It's never been done before."

- "That's ridiculous"

- "Let's be realistic."

- "That's far too difficult"

In addition the concepts of a "Tight Matrix" and "War Room" discussed in HR are tools in building effective communications within the project team.

5 Management & Communication Styles

5.1 Management Styles

Communication can be influenced by management style. One researcher describes the following management styles:

Authoritarian: Lays down strict rules and ensures that individuals know exactly what is expected of them.

Combative: Thrives on conflict. Does not mind being disagreeable.

Conciliatory: Likes to get everyone working as a team. Usually very friendly with everyone.

Disruptive: Tends to be disruptive and disorderly.

Ethical: Always honest and sincere and fair. Likes to follow the rule book.

Facilitating: Likes to delegate with a hands off approach but is available for help and guidance.
Intimidating: Projects a tough guy image and enjoys reprimanding people.

Judicial: Applies sound judgment

Promotional: Works at promoting team spirit and ensures recognition and reward for good work. Strives to ensure people realise their full potential

Secretive: Does not share information

Democratic: All decisions made jointly between manager and staff.

5.2 Communication Styles

The following communication styles shown in the table below have also been suggested.

Characteristic	Known As
Altruistic-Nurturing	Friendly helpers
	Nice people
	Warm hearted & caring
Assertive-Directive	Winners
	Go-getters
	Fighters
Analytic-Autonomising	Thinkers
	Planners
	Organisers & Analysers
Flexible-Cohering	Team Players
	Socialisers
	Flexible

6 Communication Channels

As the scope of a project grows larger, the project team tends to grow larger. The number of possible communication channels among project team members is given by the following formula:

$$n(n-1)/2$$

where "n" represents the number of people on the team.

As the team size increases the number of possible communication channels increases exponentially.

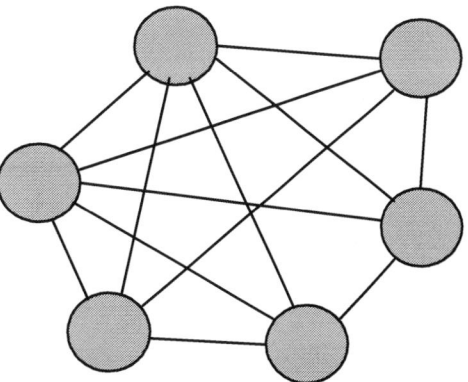

Communications Management Practice Questions

1. In the matrix form of project management the project manager must be especially adept at which form of communication?

a) Upward
b) Downward
c) Diagonal
d) Lateral

2. The communication model consists of the following components except

a) Communicator
b) Message
c) Medium
d) Facilitator

3. When preparing a presentation the most important thing to do first is to:

a) Determine the audience
b) Determine the objective
c) Decide on the overall form of the presentation
d) Examine the environment in which the presentation is to take place

4. Of the following techniques, which method decreases the effectiveness of project communication?

a) Obtaining feedback, preferably in more than one form
b) Using technical language
c) Using simple language
d) Reinforcing words with actions

5. Of the following methods that project managers use to resolve conflicts, which is the most effective for dealing with problems?

a) Confrontation
b) Compromise
c) Smoothing
d) Forcing

6. A communications barrier could be caused by which of the following?

a) Differing perceptions as to goals and objectives
b) Competition for facilities, equipment, material, manpower, and other resources
c) Personal antagonisms or personality clashes between managers and other personnel
d) All of the above

7. A group engaging in unhealthy internal competition tends to—

a) Break up and lose cohesiveness
b) Grow larger as a result of the competition
c) Grow smaller as a result of the competition
d) Become more cohesive with great internal morale

8. In the stages of group development, the emergence of trust and open communication begins in-

a) Forming
b) Norming
c) Storming
d) Performing

9. A project manager interested in supporting and developing team member confidence would use which of the following styles?

a) Assertive-directive
b) Analytical-autonomous
c) Altruistic-nurturing
d) Judicious-directive

10. Which of the following is most applicable to managing a powerful stakeholder who is not greatly concerned with the project outcome?

a) Keep satisfied
b) Manage closely
c) Monitor with minimum effort
d) Keep informed

11.Which of the following would not be done by someone who wants to be a more effective listener-

a) Watch the speaker to pick up subtle gestures and facial expressions
b) Avoid eye contact
c) Provide listener feedback
d) Take notes

12 . Most of a project managers' external communication is in the form of:-

a) Written documents
b) Oral communications
c) Informal contacts
d) Formal meetings

13. Filtering of information in the management of project communication...

a) Should be limited as much as possible
b) Is necessary for efficient communication
c) Should be imposed to make sure communications are "on message"
d) Is neither good nor bad.

14. The critical link in a project's communication is its-

a) Well-documented plan
b) Ability to computerise complex information
c) Project manager
d) Relationship to the external environment

15. Project Managers typically spend what %age of their time communicating?

a) 40 to 50
b) 75 to 90
c) 50 to 65
d) 25 to 40

16. The existence of communications barriers may result in-

a) On time, within budget project completion
b) High levels of trust and co-operation
c) High levels of conflict
d) Enhanced reputation of the project manager

17. One of the problems in the matrix organisation form is

a) Simplicity of information flow
b) Centralisation of information
c) Open, clear, and accurate information flow
d) Complexity of information flow

18. A primary cause of ineffective communication arises from differences in-

a) Message sources
b) Individual perceptions
c) Message receivers
d) Media

19. Project managers have most power in what kind of project structure?

a) Projectised
b) Strong matrix
c) Balanced matrix
d) Functional

20. In becoming an effective communicator with the project team, the project manager must understand-

a) People should be treated differently with respect to their abilities and motivation
b) People should be treated differently as they mature in their job skills
c) A single communications style will simplify project communication
d) a + b

21. The presence of communication barriers is most likely to lead to—

a) Reduced productivity
b) Increased hostility
c) Low morale
d) Increased conflict

22. The Post Project Review should address all of the following except---

a) Identifying examples of good practice
b) Recommending changes to company procedures
c) Identification of the best performing team members
d) Suggesting possible future risk mitigation strategies

23. A project manager is reporting the final status of the closed contract to the stakeholders. Which form of communication is appropriate?

a) Informal written
b) Informal verbal
c) Formal written
d) Forma verbal

24. The project manager can enhance project communication and team building by doing all the following except—

a) Having a war room
b) Being a good communication blocker
c) Being a communication expeditor
d) Holding effective meetings

25. Which of the following is not a generally recognised management style?

a) Populist
b) Combative
c) Authoritarian
d) Democratic

26. In communicating with the customer, the project manager should—

a) Be honest to the extent that the project organization is protected from litigation
b) Strive to develop a friendly, honest, and open relationship
c) Try to maximize profits by encouraging scope creep
d) Do whatever it takes to satisfy the customer and win additional business

27. Of the following factors, which one has the greatest effect on the project's communication requirements?

a) Stakeholder responsibility relationships
b) External information needs
c) Availability of technology
d) The project's organizational structure

28. In general terms disagreement amongst stakeholders should be resolved in favour of...

a) The Sponsor
b) End users
c) The Customer
d) The Performing Organisation

29. The process of conferring with others to come to terms or reach an agreement is called—

a) Win-win
b) Negotiation
c) Getting to yes
d) Confrontation

30. At the end of each project, the project team should prepare a lessons learned summary that focuses on all the following except—

a) Sharing best practices with other project teams in the organization
b) Warning others of potential problems
c) Suggesting methods to mitigate risks effectively to ensure success
d) Sharing only positive aspects of the project for future replication elsewhere in the organization

31. In the concept stage of a large road construction project you have identified a potentially powerful objector. What would be your overall strategy in relation to this person?

a) Manage closely
b) Try and prevent them from obtaining information about the project
c) Monitor with minimum effort
d) Try and get them on your side.

32. Which of the following skills is usually the most neglected aspect of communication?

a) Speaking
b) Listening
c) Writing
d) Reading

33. Which of the following statements best describes Performance Reporting?

a) The change control board receives performance reports and generates change requests to modify aspects of the project.
b) Performance reporting focuses on examining earned value analysis to determine whether cost overruns will require budget revisions.
c) Performance reporting includes status reports, which detail where the project is now; progress reports, which describe accomplishments; and forecasts, which predict future status and progress.
d) Performance reporting includes histograms, flow charts, and bar charts to show network dependencies and relationships.
e)

34. Which of the following is true regarding communication within an environment?

a) The project manager must assume the primary burden of responsibility to ensure that messages sent have been received.
b) Effective meetings, a war room, and a tight matrix promote communication.
c) If a project consists of 12 people, 48 potential channels of communication exist.
d) Most project managers spend 30 percent of their working hours engaged in communication.

35. Which of the following is not good for building effective team communications?

a) Have a War Room
b) Eliminate communication blockers
c) Have a single consistent means of communication
d) Have a meeting policy

36. Which performance reporting technique best integrates scope, cost and performance information?

a) Performance reviews
b) Variance analysis
c) Trend Analysis
d) Earned Value Analysis

PRACTICE QUESTION ANSWERS

		Page	Paragraph	
1	D	135	2.2	Lateral i.e. cross functional communication, is usually more complex than within a function.
2	D	159	1.3	
3	B			a), c) and d) will affect the way the presentation is carried out but determining the objective takes priority.
4	B	159	1.5	Before using jargon or technical language you must make sure that the recipient understands it.
5	A	144	6.3	
6	D	159	1.5	
7	A			Self evident.
8	C	140	4.3	The key word here is emergence. Trust and openness are fully present in Norming hence must emerge in Storming.
9	C	166	5.2	
10	A	161	2.3	
11	B	158	1.2	
12	A			Communication outside the project is mostly done formally in writing.
13	A	159	1.4	Filtering involves loss of data and should be avoided.
14	C			Self evident.
15	B	165	4.0	
16	C	160	1.5	
17	D	135	2.2	
18	B	159	1.5	
19	A	137	2.3	
20	D			Self evident.
21	D	160	1.5	
22	C	46	6.5	
23	C			All project reports must be communicated as formal written documents especially if contracts are involved.
24	B			Self evident.
25	A	166	5.1	
26	B			This is the only enduring strategy.
27	D			The way in which a company is organised will have the greatest effect on its communication requirements.
28	C			Whenever there is a fundamental disagreement, customer satisfaction should always prevail.
29	B			Self evident.
30	D	46	6.5	There are valuable lessons to be learned from things that went wrong.
31	A	162	2.3	
32	B	158	1.2	
33	C	164	3.3	
34	B	165	4.3	
35	C	166	4.0	
36	D	92	4.10	

Chapter 9

Project Risk Management

1 Project Risk Management Processes

1.1 Plan Risk Management

The overall planning as how to manage risk on the project.

1.2 Identify Risks

The process of identifying as many risks as possible that may affect the project outcome.

1.3 Perform Qualitative Risk Analysis

Carrying out a qualitative analysis of the probability and possible impact of each risk so as to prioritise them for further analysis.

1.4 Perform Quantitative Analysis

Attempting to numerically quantify the effects of individual risks on the project outcome.

1.5 Plan Risk Response

Developing responses that will mitigate threats and enhance opportunities.

1.6 Monitor and Control Risk Response

The tracking of identified risks, executing and monitoring risk responses and measuring their effectiveness and identifying new risks throughout the project life cycle.

2 Approach to this module

Project Risk Management consists of all those processes concerned with the identification and analysis of risk and the development of responses to specific risk events.

This Chapter will first cover the fundamentals of risk not adequately addressed by the *PMBOK® Guide* and will then concentrate on a more detailed treatment of the process and the principal tools and techniques.

3 Understanding the Meaning of Risk

Before examining the Risk processes it is useful to examine what we mean by risk.

3.1 The Two Definitions of Risk

The *PMBOK® Guide* defines risk in two different ways.

Firstly risk is thought of as uncertainty. In other words a risk event can have a negative or a positive outcome. In the second definition risk is thought of as a threat, and the only possible outcomes are either neutral or negative. PMI tends to lean to the former view which means that risk has both a downside as well as an upside.

The *PMBOK® Guide* states that:-

 "Project risk management objectives are to increase the probability and impact of positive events and decrease and decrease the probability of negative events in the project."

Downside risks are often referred to as **threats** whilst upside risks are **opportunities.**

3.2 The Two Risk Types

There are two main classes of risk:

1. **Business risks:** Those normal risks of doing business that can result in either gain or loss. (Sometimes referred to as **Direct** risks)

2. **Pure, or insurable risks**: Those risks if they materialise can only result in loss. Examples are:-

- Direct damage to property
- Indirect consequential loss such as loss of business and clean up costs due for instance to fire or flood.
- Legal liabilities to third parties

If you can take out insurance against a risk then you need not actively manage it. Insurance is a type of risk transfer, which leaves you to focus your efforts on the business risks.

3.3 Risk Factors

Risk is characterised by 3 factors:

1. **Risk event**: What might happen to the benefit or detriment of the project.
2. **Risk probability**: The likelihood of occurrence of the event.
3. **Amount at stake**: The extent of loss or gain that could result

   Exposure = Risk probability x Amount at stake

3.4 Risk & the Project Life Cycle

The time to address risk is at the start of a project. This is the point when the number of unknowns, i.e. the risk, is greatest but the amount at stake, i.e. money invested, is the lowest. This is illustrated below.

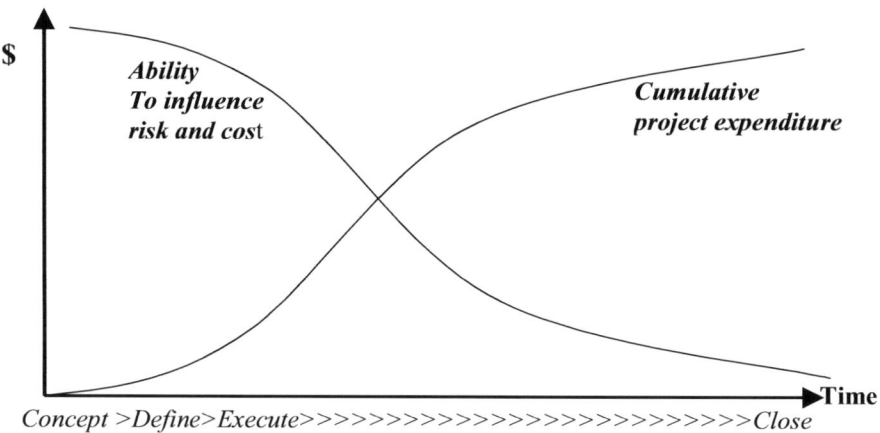

4 Plan Risk Management

This is the process of deciding how to approach and plan the overall risk management activities of the project.

The **Risk Management Plan,** which is the only output of risk management planning, describes generally how risk items will be identified, analysed and controlled.

The principal input to the Risk Management Plan is the **Project Scope Statement**.

Note that the plan does *not* identify specific risks. It defines the approach to risk management.

Risk Management Plan Contents

- Methodology
    - o Approach, tools, techniques
- Roles and responsibilities
    - o Clarifies responsibilities
- Budget
    - o Cost of Risk Management process
- Timing
    - o When and how often Risk Management cycle will be performed
- Risk Categories
    - o How the risk areas will be broken down e.g Risk Breakdown Structure

- Definition of Risk Probability and Impact
  - o Applying quantitative scales to probability and impact
- Probability and Impact Matrix (see later)
- How risks will be reported and tracked

5 Identify Risks

5.1 Risk identification

The process of determining which risk events might affect the project   i.e. what can go wrong and what opportunities are there to improve matters. This can be looked at on two levels.

1. Potential generic sources of risk such as schedule, cost, technical, legal. etc.
2. Specific risk events

Risk identification is not a once off activity. It should be carried out at the start of the project and then reviewed regularly throughout the project life cycle as part of risk monitoring and control.

5.2 Defining a risk

Poor definition of project risks makes subsequent analysis more difficult. For instance saying that a project may be late is not much use as a statement of risk. Being late is a consequence of many possible risks. In order to be able to address a risk you must state it in the form of risk, cause and consequence.

1. What the **risk** is.
2. Which would **cause** the risk
3. What would be the **consequence**s of it happening.

The following is a good example of defining a risk.

*There is a **risk** that our customer will be unable to complete acceptance tests in a timely fashion, **caused** by their lack of experience in procuring this type of equipment, **resulting** in delayed payment, project overrun, and delayed initiation of support contracts*

5.3 Tools & Techniques for Risk Identification

1) Brainstorming
This is the most used tool and is best carried out by the project team with appropriate stakeholders and subject matter experts.

2) Work Breakdown Structure
Because the WBS defines all the project work and hence all the deliverables a lot of possible risks can be identified by analysing at task level.

3) SWOT Analysis

SWOT stands for Strengths, Weaknesses, Opportunities and Threats. Strengths and Opportunities generate upside risks. Weaknesses and Threats identify downside risks. SWOT can be used to give structure to Brainstorming.

4) Assumptions analysis

Reviewing all the assumptions made in project planning to see if any of them constitute a risk.

5) Checklist Analysis

Using existing prompt sheets and check lists to identify further risks

6) Delphi Technique

A facilitator solicits information regarding significant project risks. The contributors independently arrive at their conclusions and the facilitator consolidates all the opinions and recirculates the information for further comment. The process stops when consensus is reached or it becomes apparent that it will never be reached. The purpose of this process is to avoid individuals having undue influence.

7) Root Cause Identification

It may be possible to trace several different risks to the same root cause. Hence addressing that root cause will hopefully address several risks.

8) Cause and Effect analysis

This was addressed in section 5.3 of Quality Management

9) Expert judgement

Canvassing the views of subject matter experts or people with relevant experience.

10) Flow charts

Flow charts show how components interact and thus may help in identifying causes of risk.

11) Influence diagrams

An influence diagram is a visual representation of a problem requiring decisions for its solution. An arrow denotes influence. For instance the simple example below shows for instance, that sales volume is influenced by quality and by unit price.

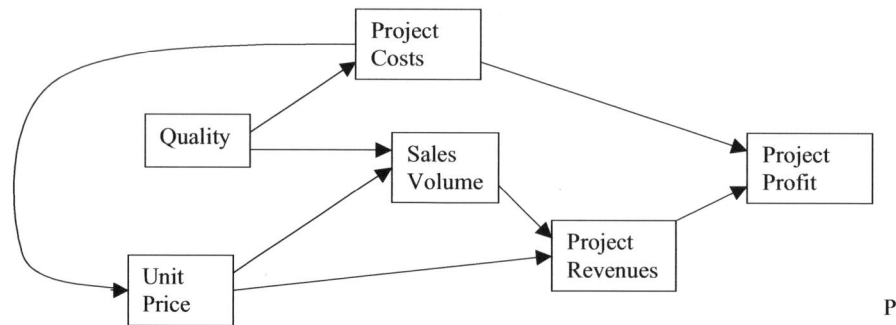

5.4 Risk Register

The primary output of risk identification is the Risk Register. The register will intimately maintain all the information pertaining to each identified risk but at this stage is little more than a list and the next step is to try and quantify the risks so as to prioritise them.

6 Perform Qualitative Risk Analysis

This is about prioritising the potential impact of each identified risk in terms of the probable effect on project objectives. A simple tool with wide application in industry and commerce is the Probability/Impact Matrix shown below.

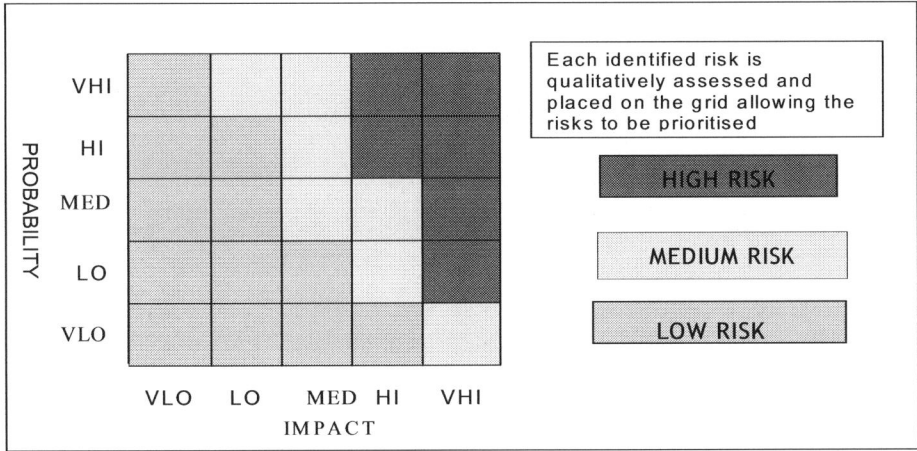

A pseudo quantitative method often used is to simply apply a scale of 1 to 5 to the impact and probability. Multiplying these scales gives the Exposure for each square that can be used to prioritise the risks.

Exposure = Probability x Impact

A drawback of this method is that it gives the same weight to both probability and impact whereas in reality high impact is more serious than high probability. High impact items must be addressed even if they have low probability. The shading in the grid is a better representation of the relative importance.

	1	2	3	4	5
5	5	10	15	20	25
4	4	8	12	16	20
3	3	6	9	12	15
2	2	4	6	8	10
1	1	2	3	4	5

7 Perform Quantitative Risk Analysis

This process analyses numerically the probability and impact of each risk and the consequences for project objectives. In particular it:-

1. Estimates the probability of achieving a specific project objective.

2. Quantifies the risk exposure and determines the size of schedule and cost contingencies.

3. Identifies the risks requiring most attention.

4. Identifies realistic project goals.

There are a variety of tools to help us do this.

7.1 Probability and Impact Matrix

An important reason for carrying out risk analysis is to allocate money in the budget to cover risk. To do this the qualitative scales used above must be converted to actual probabilities and costs. Thus for each identified risk we will calculate an estimate of the exposure. This is not easy to do but estimates have to be made in order to quantify, in monetary terms, the potential impact on the project.

7.2 Decision Tree Analysis

The use of decision trees requires an appreciation of the concept of **expected value**. The concept is very similar to exposure and is best illustrated with an example.

Imagine buying a sweepstake ticket for £1.

There are two possible prizes. 0.5% of tickets pay out £100. 2% pay out £10 and the remaining 97.5% pay nothing.

This is summarised as follows:

Prize Value	Probability of Winning	Average Return
£100.00	0.005	50p
£10.00	0.020	20p
£0.00	0.975	0
Total	1.00	70p

The Average Return is the Prize Value times the Probability of Winning.
If we add up the average returns we get 70 pence.

This is the average outcome for any single bet. This is called the Expected Value.

Note that we can never win the expected value on a single bet. However if we repeated the bet many times we would on average receive 70P for every pound wagered.

Be aware that in a project environment Expected Value is a statistical assessment of project value, not a prediction of final revenue or cost and we would not expect to base decisions purely on this statistic.

7.3 Decision-Tree Example

Decision-tree analysis attempts to break down a series of events into smaller, simpler, and more manageable segments. Once again the concept is best illustrated by an example.

Your project requires 500 ruggedised computers. Your supplier has a history of quality problems. The decision to take is whether or not to commission tests of the computers before site installation. The following data is available:

- Historical failure rate of SW is 4%
- Tests will cost £6000 per module
- Cost of repairing failed units in house is £10,000
- Cost of repairing installed units is £200,000

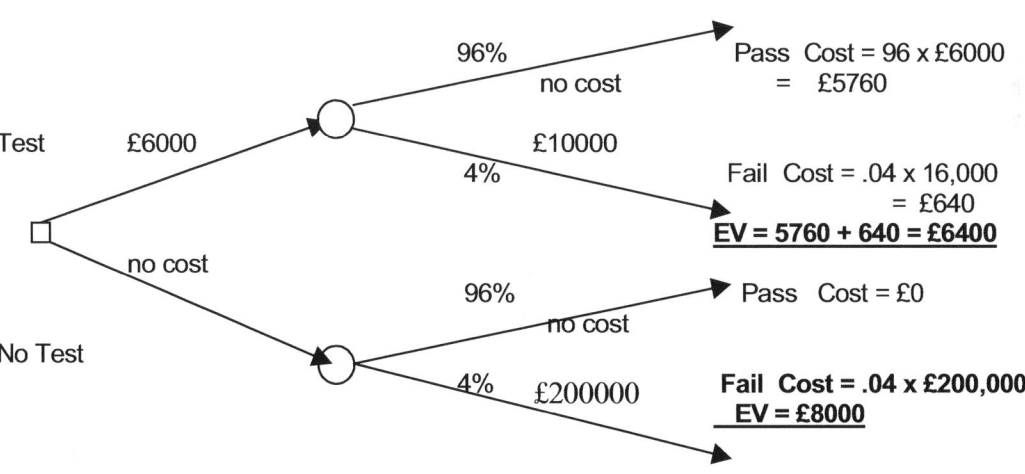

In this example there is an initial decision point, test or not test, followed by all possible outcomes. The expected value of each decision is calculated by summing up the expected value of each possible output for that decision.

7.4 Monte Carlo Analysis

Monte Carlo Analysis, covered in Project Time Management, is an important tool for risk quantification especially with regard to schedule risk. Although much more difficult to apply it is considered a superior approach to analysing the schedule than PERT or CPM. This is because PERT and CPM fail to account for path convergence (see below) and thus tend to underestimate project durations. Most scheduling software (e.g. Microsoft Project) use a single duration value for each activity to calculate the critical path. Some packages use the Monte Carlo method. This method utilises all three PERT values i.e. optimistic, expected and pessimistic. PERT itself simply uses the PERT formulae to produce a single value (see Chapter 4).

The Monte Carlo method works by sampling each activity duration from the probability distribution determined by the 3 values. It does this many times so that instead of producing a single value for the project duration it produces a probability distribution. (see figure on page 69).

It thus gives a quantitative assessment of the overall risk, both upside and downside, to the project end date.

7.5 Path Convergence

Consider the situation below.

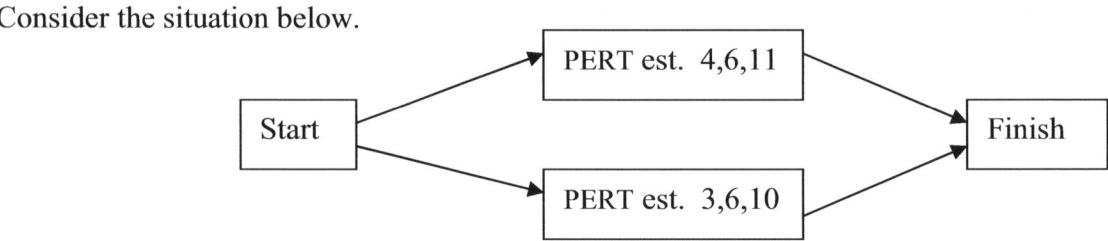

If both activities took their expected durations then the duration of this network segment would be 6 units. However suppose that the upper activity performed well and took 4 days whilst the lower activity performed less well and took 7 days. Both are well within the PERT limits. However the overall duration is now 7 units. Thus no matter how well some activities perform the worst performing path will determine the schedule. Where paths converge the benefits of early completion are lost.

7.6 Sensitivity Analysis

This attempts to analyse the effect of a change to a single variable within a project. Risk is reflected by defining possible ranges in outcomes and measuring their effect. So seeing how sensitive the possible outcomes are to changes in variables. e.g. interest rates.

7.7 Interviewing and Expert Judgement

Views can be gained by interviewing stakeholders and subject matter experts.

8 Plan Risk Response

Risk Response Planning involves defining ways to enhance opportunities and reduce threats.

8.1 Responses to Negative Risks (Threats)

Avoid the threat.

This strategy might be chosen if a particular risk event is simply not acceptable, for example a risk may have severe, or disastrous consequences even though its probability may not be high. A useful tool whenever this happens is to adopt an alternative strategy. That is, find another approach to get the job done or just do not do at all, even if it means abandoning the project.

Accept or retain the risk.

In this case, the risk is acceptable (low probability, low impact) and you decide not to worry about it. Proceed with the project and take the risk; if the risk event occurs, you can live with it. However this does not mean you can totally ignore such risks. You still need to calculate the total exposure and include a suitable amount of contingency in the budget.

Mitigate, control, or reduce the risk.

Mitigation involves including actions within the project plan to reduce the probability of the risk happening and/or its impact if it does. i.e. reduce the exposure. Another form of mitigation is putting **contingency plans** in place, such that if the risk event does occur, its impact has been lessened. An example popular with the IT industry is **Escrow**, the regular placing of updated copies of developing software with a third party.

Note that the exposure after mitigation must be included in the budget.

Deflect or transfer the risk.

There are several ways in which you can attempt to pass the risk to another party:

- Purchase insurance or use a performance bond
- Use a warranty
- Use a subcontractor with back-to-back agreement e.g passing penalties imposed by the client on to the subcontractors.
- Use of different contract types (this is fully covered in Procurement Management)

Share the risk.

When there are several parties to a contract often the best approach to risk is to share it. As a general guide, the party who is the source of a particular risk, and/or the party in the best position to control it is the one who should bear the greatest part.

Contingency Reserve

The use of a reserve is another way to reduce or mitigate the impact of cost and schedule overruns on specific project risks or on unidentified risks. Refer to Project Cost Management for a description of the two major types of reserves.

8.2 Responses to Positive Risks (Opportunities)

Exploit/Enhance

Make the most of any opportunity by for instance allocating more budget or resources or giving it more management attention.

Share

Examples of sharing are bringing in a third party with more expertise, or forming a joint venture company.

Accept

As for negative risks we can just accept the situation but not actively pursue it.

9 Risk Monitoring & Control

9.1 Risk Management

Each risk that has a planned response must be proactively managed by the person responsible. In addition the risk plan need to be formally reviewed on a regular basis.

The situation is bound to change because:-

- Some risks mature into problems (issues)
- Some risks are resolved or do not arise
- Probability/impacts change; up or down
- New risks arise that were not identified initially
- Project scope changes give new risk opportunities

Thus, Risk Monitoring & Control consists of:

- Keeping track of identified risks
- Executing risk plans

- Monitoring residual risks (risk that remains after risk responses have been implemented)
- Identifying new risks
- Evaluating effectiveness of risk plan

The primary tool for keeping track of project risk is the **Risk Register** an example of which is shown below.

Project _____ Prepared by: _____ Reference:_____ Date:_____							
Key: H - High, M - Medium, L - Low							
Risk ID	Description	Prob H M L	Impact Cost Time		Response Strategy	Effect	Risk Owner

Some companies also maintain a "Watchlist" where they record low exposure risks that have been accepted but do not warrant inclusion on the risk register.

We can make use of the following tools.

9.2 Project risk response audits.

Risk auditors examine and document the effectiveness of the risk response in avoiding, transferring, or mitigating risk occurrence as well as the effectiveness of the risk owner. Risk audits are performed during the project life cycle to control risk.

9.3 Periodic project risk reassessment

Project risk reviews should be regularly scheduled. Project risk should be an agenda item at all team meetings. Risk ratings and prioritisation may change during the life of the project. Any changes may require additional qualitative or quantitative analysis.

9.4 Earned value analysis.

Earned value is used for monitoring overall project performance against a baseline plan. Results from an earned value analysis may indicate potential deviation of the project at completion from cost and schedule targets. When a project deviates significantly from the baseline, updated risk identification and analysis should be performed.

9.5 Technical performance measurement.

Technical performance measurement compares technical accomplishments during project execution to the project plan's schedule of technical achievement. Deviation, such as not demonstrating functionality as planned at a milestone, can imply a risk to achieving the project's scope.

9.6 Reserve Analysis

As risk events (both upside and downside risks) occur they will consume or increase the contingency reserves. Reserve analysis consists of analysing the current level of the reserves to see if they need to be increased or conversely, if funds can be released.

9.7 Workarounds

When a negative risk event occurs that was not expected, or for which no mitigation plan has been formulated, or for which the planned mitigation has failed, then additional response panning must be carried out immediately. This is known as a workaround.

Risk Management Practice Questions

1. Which of the following statements best describes the general principle of fairness in risk allocation regarding contracts?

a. The party who has the most knowledge of certain risks and is in the best position to minimise those risks should bear most, if not all, of those risks.
b. The party who can gain whatever competitive advantage exists as a result of certain risks not occurring should bear most, if not all, of those risks.
c. The greater the number of risks, the better it is to share risks among all contractual parties.
d. The seller must always bear more risk than the buyer, because the seller is the one party to the contract who is getting reimbursed for the work performed.

2. If a risk event has a 90 percent chance of occurring and the impact will be $10,000, what does $9,000 represent?

a. Risk value
b. Expected value
c. Real value
d. Contingency budget

3. The Delphi method was developed as a means to gather information from "experts" for decision making. All the below listed characteristics are found in this technique except—

a. A panel of experts is identified
b. Panel members should not know each other's identity, at least initially
c. A facilitator co-ordinates and compiles the information
d. The facilitator will terminate the process only when unanimity of opinion is achieved

4. A "business risk"—

a. Only has a loss associated with it
b. Only has a gain associated with it
c. Can be mitigated through insurance
d. Has the potential for both gain and loss

5. The first activity performed in the risk management process is risk—

a. Calculation
b. Planning
c. Identification
d. Analysis

6. Which of the following would you not expect to find in a Risk Management Plan

a. Risk methodology
b. Risk Categories
c. Responses to specific risks
d. How risks will be tracked

7. A key objective of risk quantification is to—

a. Improve the accuracy of risk assessment
b. Take the guesswork out of the risk management process
c. Compare the cost of risk response development to the risk's expected monetary value
d. Facilitate the quantification of cost contingencies

8. When putting risks in priority order, clearly the risks that should be on the top are those that—

a. Will have both the highest probability of occurrence and the greatest impact
b. Have the highest probability of occurrence regardless of impact
c. Will affect safety regardless of cost and schedule
d. Have the greatest impact regardless of probability of occurrence

9. The project risk management processes can be summarised as:-

a. Planning, identifying, quantifying, mitigating and tracking
b. Planning, identifying, analysing, response planning and controlling
c. Planning identifying, categorising, mitigating and controlling
d. Planning mitigating, avoiding, accepting, deflecting

10. The *ultimate* responsibility for identifying risks to a project and deciding their subsequent treatment rests with the—

a. Project sponsor
b. Project manager
c. Project team
d. Project manager and project sponsor

11. Project risk management includes the principle objective of—

a. Ensuring that negative events don't occur
b. Ensuring that positive events do occur
c. Planning that negative and positive events negate each other through diligent risk management practices
d. Maximising the results of positive events and minimising the consequences of adverse events

12. Project risk is characterised by which of the following three factors:

a. Severity of impact, duration of impact, cost of impact
b. Identification, type of risk category, probability of impact
c. Risk event, risk probability, the amount at stake
d. Occurrence, frequency, cost

13. A risk event is the precise description of what might happen to the _____ of the project.

a. Detriment and benefit
b. Detriment
c. Risk profile
d. Budget

14. Which of the following are possible strategies for handling positive risk?

a. subcontract the work
b. increase the budget
c. add resource
d. all are possible strategies

15. The project budget is set for the total project. There is some work that has not been identified in the initial planning, which must be accomplished. The most appropriate source of funds to cover this work is the

a. Management Reserve
b. Contingency reserve
c. Slush fund reserve
d. Contract reserve

16. The risk management process has identified 120 risks with an average probability of 2% and an average impact of $8000. It has been decided to accept all the risks without individual mitigation. How much contingency should be added to the budget?

a. $192,000
b. $19,200
c. $1,920
d. none of the above

17. At what stage in the project life cycle does the project manager have the most ability to influence total costs

a. Concept
b. Definition
c. Execution
d. Closing

18. Workarounds are

a. Unplanned responses to negative risk events
b. Outputs from risk response development
c. The same as contingency plans
d. Inputs to risk response control

19. Which of the following are classified as Business Risks?

a. Liability loss
b. Direct property loss
c. Profit loss
d. Personnel related loss

20. When performing a risk analysis, of the following, which is the most effective tool for ensuring that as many risks as possible are identified?

a. WBS
b. Milestone plan
c. The project schedule
d. Project checklist

21. Where would a project manager least like to find risk on a project

a. Financing
b. Technical
c. Safety
d. Security

22. Risk management is applied throughout the life of a project. How should a project manager best accommodate unforeseen risks:

a. Ignore the possibility until it happens
b. Transfer all risks to the sponsor
c. Based on experience - contingency allowances are made
d. A person is detailed to continually monitor risks

23.   Which of the following describes reserve analysis

a.   Deciding on the required amount of management reserve
b.   Deciding on the required amount of contingency reserve
c.   Seeing if the remaining reserves are sufficient for project completion
d.   None of the above

24. Additional risk response planning is *especially* needed when the—

a.   Project is slipping
b.   Cost baseline is changed
c.   A risk event was unexpected or the effect was greater than forecast
d.   Project plan is updated

25.   In a proactive approach to project risk management, the amount of a contingency reserve should be based on—

a.   Percentages based on past experience
b.   The sum total of the most likely probability and impact of the various risk events
c.   A set amount allocated to each item proportionately
d.   An allowance of 10% for each phase in the project life cycle

26. An example of risk mitigation is—

a.   Using performance and payment bonds
b.   Eliminating a specific threat by eliminating the cause
c.   Avoiding the schedule risk inherent in the project
d.   Reducing the expected monetary value of a risk event by reducing the probability of occurrence

27. On a typical project, when are risks highest and impacts (amount at stake) lowest?

a.   During the concept phase
b.   At or near completion of the project
c.   During the implementation phase
d.   When the project manager is replaced

28. Which of the following is an example of an external risk?

a.   Poor staff assignments
b.   Incorrect cost estimates
c.   Inflation
d.   Contract type

29. The highest risk impact generally occurs during which of the following project life-cycle phases?

a. Concept and planning
b. Planning and implementation
c. Implementation and closeout
d. Concept and closeout

30. In risk response control, corrective action consists primarily of—

a. Performing the planned risk response
b. Changing the schedule and cost baselines
c. Updating estimates of probability and value
d. Updating the risk management plan

31. Of the four main areas of risk inherent in projects, which one will have the most lasting impact if not managed well?

a. Scope risk
b. Schedule risk
c. Cost risk
d. Quality risk

32. The most important aspects of a risk from a project management point of view are its—

a. Causes
b. Effects
c. Costs
d. Exposure value

33. All the following are purposes of project risk management except—

a. Identifying factors that are likely to affect the project scope, quality, time, and cost
b. Developing response strategies for all identified risks
c. Providing a baseline for project factors that cannot be controlled
d. Mitigating impacts by influencing project factors that can be controlled

34. Which of the following is not an objective of a risk audit?

a. Confirming that risk management processes have been adhered to
b. Confirming that risks are being controlled
c. Identifying new potential risks to the project
d. Ensuring that major risks have been quantified and mitigated

35. Contingency planning involves—

a. Defining the steps to be taken if an identified risk event should occur
b. Establishing a management reserve to cover unplanned expenditures
c. Preparing a stand-alone document that is separate from the overall project plan
d. Determining needed adjustments to make during the implementation phase of a project

36. Which of the following tools is the most appropriate for measuring schedule risk?

a. CPM
b. Monte Carlo
c. PERT
d. PDM

PRACTICE QUESTION ANSWERS

		Page	Paragraph	
1	A	187	8.1	
2	B	184	7.2	
3	D	182	5.3	
4	D	179	3.2	
5	B	178	1.1	
6	C	180	4	
7	D	184	7	Unless we quantify the risk exposure we cannot allocate a meaningful cost contingency
8	C			Self evident
9	B	178	1	
10	A			The PM will manage the process and evaluate the risk options but ultimate responsibility lies with the person whose money is at risk.
11	D	187	8	
12	C	179	3.3	
13	A	179	3.2	This is in accord with the definition of business risk
14	D	188	8.2	
15	A	96	7.2	Work not identified on the WBS has not been included in the baseline budget or the contingency reserve.
16	B	179	3.3	Total exposure = 120 x 2% x $8,000 = $19,200
17	A	180	3.4	
18	A	190	9.7	
19	C	179	3.2	
20	A	181	5.3	As has been said previously, when in doubt the WBS is most often the required answer
21	C			Self evident
22	C	96	7.2	
23	C	190	9.6	
24	C	190	9.7	
25	B	179	3.3	
26	D	187	8.1	
27	A	180	3.4	
28	C			Self evident
29	C	180	3.4	The impact of a risk event is highest when work has already been started or completed
30	A	189	9.1	
31	D			After a project is completed a), b) and c) are history but poor quality will not go away
32	A			Prevention is better than cure
33	C			Self evident (c is nonsense)
34	C	189	9.2	
35	A	187	8.1	
36	B	186	7.4	

Chapter 10

Project Procurement Management

Project Procurement Management Processes

Procurement Management involves those processes required to acquire goods and services required for the project, from outside suppliers. The processes are:-

1 Plan Procurement

Documenting the project purchasing requirements and identifying potential suppliers.

2 Conduct Procurement

The selection of sellers and the negotiating and awarding of contracts.

3 Administer Procurement

Management of suppliers and amending of contracts as required

4 Close Procurement

Closing down of contracts after completion

The remainder of this Chapter will describe this four step Procurement Process, concentrating on those areas where the *PMBOK® Guide* treatment is of insufficient depth.

Step 1: Plan Procurement

Procurement Planning is the process of determining which of the requirement for goods and/or services of the project are best satisfied by external procurement rather than internal production. Thus the key decision to take is Make or Buy. If there are no Buy decisions then there is no procurement cycle. If there are Buy decisions then we apply the procurement cycle.

Also during this step bid documents are prepared and award evaluation criteria are developed.

1.1 Make-or-buy analysis

Make or buy analysis should include the following factors.

1. The direct costs of a prospective procurement.

2. The indirect costs – i.e. the cost of managing and monitoring the purchasing process

3. The overall effect of the decision on the organisation e.g. would a decision to **Make** have a knock on effect on other projects that may require the *same* resources.

1.2 Inputs to Plan Procurement

PMBOK® Guide lists many items as inputs to the Procurement Planning process (section 12.1.1), far too many to memorise. However as the purpose of this stage is to decide what to buy and how to buy it, the inputs reflect virtually the entire project information available including stakeholder requirements, risk register, resource plan, schedule and budget. The most important input is the specification.

1.3 Outputs

The principal outputs from the Procurement Planning process are

1. Procurement Management Plan
2. Procurement Statement of Work for all items to be procured.
3. Procurement Document Package (bid documents)
4. Source selection criteria

Procurement Management Plan

The purpose of the Procurement Management Plan is to describe how the procurement process will be managed. Because the procurement process has contractual and legal implications it is a mandatory requirement that the processes that are followed are legally correct and are seen to be open, consistent and fair. A full list of possible contents is given in the (*PMBOK® Guide* section 12.1.3), but the plan should reflect the needs of each particular project

Procurement Statement of Work

The statement of work describes the item(s) to be procured in sufficient detail to allow sellers to be able to decide if they are able to supply it. It is based on the specification but would include descriptions of any connected requirement such as warranty and support requirements. The level of detail in the statement of work will depend upon the intended contract type. In general terms a fixed price contract will require a detailed specification whereas a cost plus contract can be less detailed. (see later)

Procurement Document Package

A wide variety of terms are used to describe procurement documents and there are no agreed standards. The following are widely used.

An **Invitation to Bid** is often used for routine items where the primary objective is to find the best price. The required goods and services must be clearly and accurately specified. There may or may not be negotiations and the lowest price normally wins although other factors may also influence the award.

A Request for Quotation is usually used for the purchase of commodity type items.

A Request for Proposal sometimes called an **Invitation to Tender** is used for complex, usually non-standard items, of high value. Negotiations and discussion are invariably part of the process. Whatever it is called the Procurement Document Package will contain the statement of work and a description of exactly how and when and in what form the response should be made.

Source Selection Criteria

Purchasers may receive a large number of replies so they need an objective method of comparing prospective suppliers. Evaluation Criteria are used to score and compare competing proposals.

Such criteria may include -

- Understanding of Requirements
- Overall or life-cycle costs
- Technical capability of the seller
- Financial standing
- Sellers track record
- Sellers industry knowledge
- Ability to deliver to schedule
- Quality Processes
- PMP Certification

1.4 Contract Types and the Spectrum of Risk

PMI attaches great importance to contract types and the degree of risk between buyer and seller. Both buyer and seller are attempting to minimise their exposure to risk and place most risk with the other party.

The two extremes of contracting are Cost Plus, and Firm Fixed Price, which place all the risk with the Buyer and Seller respectively. Between these two extremes is a spectrum of risk, illustrated below.

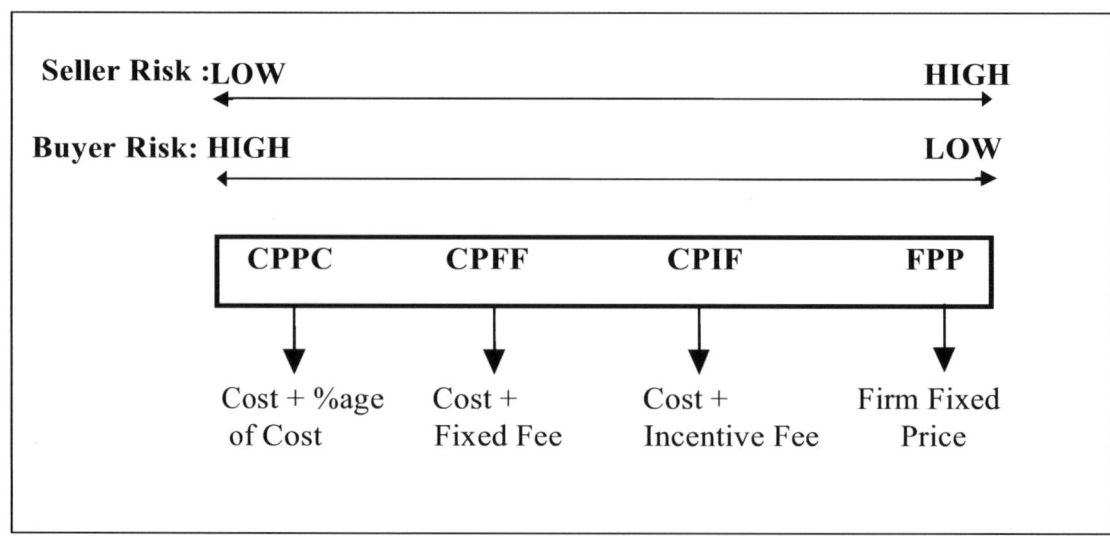

There are 3 kinds of **Cost Plus** contracts. They are collectively known as **Cost Reimbursable**.

Cost Plus Percentage of Cost (CPPC)

With a CPPC contract the seller is reimbursed for all costs, both direct and indirect, incurred in providing the goods or services contracted for. In addition there is an agreed-upon percentage of the cost as profit. The seller is obligated only to make best effort to fulfil the contract within the estimated amount. If the seller fails to do this the buyer funds all overruns. The agreed upon %age infers an "open book" approach. When "open book" does not apply it is usually referred to as Time & Materials. However in terms of allocation of Risk the two are identical.

Cost Plus Fixed Fee (CPFF)

With a CPFF contract costs are reimbursed as above but instead of adding a %age mark up there is a fixed fee that is paid in instalments as the contract progresses. Although there is a ceiling on the seller's profit, there is no great motivation to control costs, so that most risk remains with the buyer. However this can be an unsatisfactory contract for the seller as an overrun will reduce the margin % even though the £margin is fixed.

Cost Plus Incentive Fee (CPIF)

With a CPIF contract costs are reimbursed as in the above examples and there is also a predetermined fee as for CPFF. However if actual cost varies from the expected cost, then the buyer and seller share in the savings or overruns based on a predetermined share ratio, often 50/50 though other ratios may be used. Effectively, an incentive fee is agreed for performance to plan. The fee is decreased for under performance and increased for over performance in line with the share ratio.

Example: A contract is agreed for 150 days effort where the price is £1000/day and the target incentive fee is   £50,000.

Thus target price =   £150,000
                +   __50,000__
                =   £200,000   equivalent to £1,333/day

Outcome1: job takes 120 days

Cost saving = 30 days = £30,000

Actual price = 120 x £1000   = £120,000
+ fee   =   50,000
+ share of saving   =   __15,000__
                                 £185,000   equivalent to £1,541/day

Client has saved £15,000, Seller has increased day rate hence shared benefit.

Outcome 2: job takes 170 days

Cost overrun = 20 days = £20,000

Actual price = 170 x £1000	= £170,000	
+fee	= 50,000	
- share of overrun	= -10,000	
Total price	= £210,000	equivalent to £1,235/day

Client has spent extra £10,000, Seller has reduced day rate so penalty shared.

Firm Fixed Price (FFP)

With a FFP contract the seller furnishes goods or services at a fixed price regardless as to how much it cost to provide them. Thus the seller bears all the risk. For such contracts the seller will normally build in cost contingencies and include a risk premium. If risks are well controlled there is a greater profit potential than for cost reimbursable projects. This approach is best suited for situations were the specifications are well defined and costs are predictable. For less predictable situations a wise seller will increase his risk premium.

On some contracts it is permissible for the supplier to increase the contract price if the price of agreed commodities or labour rises, according to a specified index. Such contracts are normally called **Fixed Price** rather than Firm Fixed Price. PMI use the rather long winded Fixed Price with Economic Price Adjustment (FP-EPA)

1.5 Contract Origination (Unilateral/Bilateral)

Contracts can either be *Unilateral* or *Bilateral*. A *Bilateral* contract is initiated via a request for quotations, request for proposals or invitations to bid and always involves negotiation.

A Unilateral contract takes the form of a purchase order for standard items at standard prices, usually taken from a catalogue or price list. There can be bulk-buying discounts and some buyers will have individually negotiated discount agreements. These are sometimes called unit Price contracts or Frame Agreements. The vendor usually accepts the purchase order automatically. Unilateral contracts issued in this way normally do not involve any negotiation.

If a purchase order is sent to a prospective supplier then there is no contract between the parties until either of the following takes place.

1. The supplier acknowledges the purchase order and agrees to its terms
2. The supplier commences to deliver goods or services.

1.6 Contract Incentives

Incentives to perform are an important element of any contract. Incentives can be positive i.e. a "carrot", or negative, i.e. a "stick". The incentive fees discussed earlier are a form of carrot. Penalty clauses are a form of *stick*. Experience has shown that a good balance of *carrot* and *stick* can be beneficial and cost effective for both parties. Contract incentives can be applied to both parties to a contract, their primary purpose being to try and align the needs of both buyer and seller.

Step 2: Conduct Procurement

This step involves receiving responses from interested parties, selecting the suppliers with the best offering, using the previously defined selection criteria, and then negotiating a contract with them.

2.1 Tools & Techniques for Conduct Procurement

Qualified Seller List.

This is contained within the Procurement Plan. In order to determine whether a potential vendor is a suitable supplier factors such as the following need to be considered

- Financial status of seller
- Seller Industry Knowledge
- Delivery Capability
- Quality System
- Supplier's experience in this kind of work
- Quality of previous work
- Availability of reference sites
- Project Management Capability

Bidders Conference

It is a mandatory requirement that the tendering process must be seen to be open and fair to all potential bidders. This requires that all bidders must be given exactly the same information on which to base their bid. Information given to one must be given to all. Even with well prepared bid documents there will be ambiguities and differences in interpretation. Any such problems can be addressed at a Bidders Conference where all potential suppliers can attend and ask questions. If this is impractical the conference could be web based.

Weighting system

A weighting system for attaching relative importance to the evaluation criteria will make selection more objective and less subject to personal prejudice. An example is shown opposite.

	Score 1-5	Weight 1-5	Total
Life Cycle Costs	5	5	25
Seller Capability	1	4	4
Financial Status of Seller	3	3	9
Seller Track record	1	3	3
Seller Industry Knowledge	1	2	2
Delivery Capability	5	5	25
Quality System	2	2	4
Project Management	5	4	20
		Total	92

Such a method will also help to demonstrate that the selection process has been fair and objective.

Screening system

Establishing minimum mandatory requirements will screen out unsuitable applicants. Failure to comply with mandatory requirements means automatic elimination.

Independent Estimate/Expert Judgement

The Procurement organisation can obtain its own estimate for comparison with the contractor proposal either carrying out the estimate itself or consulting external experts.

Advertising/Internet Search

The list of potential suppliers can be extended by advertising in trade journals etc. In some instances this can be a legal requirement especially for Government contracts. Where the requirements are for commodity items then the internet can indicates possible suppliers.

2.2 Non-competitive contracts (Sole Source contracts)

Buyers always like to have a competitive situation between prospective suppliers. However, on occasions a Buyer may place a contract with a Sole Source without a competitive tender. e.g

- Where there is only one practical supplier of the goods or services required.
- When there compelling urgency
- National Security
- Public interest

Buyers must take care when placing sole source contracts to protect themselves from possible allegations of favouritism.

2.3 Contract Negotiation

The five stages of negotiation:

Contract negotiations can take place at a single meeting but are normally extended over several meetings. Whatever the time span, the following stages are passed through.

1. **Protocol:** Formal introductions
2. **Probing:** Probe each other's areas of weakness and establish the issues.
3. **Scratch bargaining:** Make agreements. Give and take.
4. **Closure:** Summarise and finalise agreements.
5. **Agreement**: Document the final agreement

2.4 Sources of Power in Negotiations

- **Need**--The Salesman needs a booking. The customer needs a solution
- **Insight** – Insight into the other person's world

- **Options**-- Does the buyer have other options? Do you have other opportunities?
- **Price, Time and Money Pressure**--Who needs a deal most?
- **Relationships**—Is there rapport & trust?
- **Investment**—Who has made the most investment to date?
- **Expectation**-What expectations are pre-set?
- **Planning & Preparation**
- **Negotiation Skill**

2.5 Negotiation tactics

- **Price**: Your price is too high
- **Fait accompli**: Claiming that a topic of dispute has already been decided or accomplished and cannot be changed
- **Limited authority**: Claiming not to have the authority to finalise the agreement just reached.
- **Foggy memory**: I can't recall saying that.
- **Fair and reasonable**: Offering comparisons to other situations, for example, to show that the price offered is reasonable
- **Deadline**: Imposing a deadline for reaching an agreement
- **Violins**: e.g. we are having a bad time and can't afford your price
- **Surprise**: Taking the other party by surprise with new information
- **Budget limit:** We can't pay more than …..
- **Carrot**: If we can agree a good deal here there will be much more business later on.
- **Ultimatum:** Take it or leave it.
- **Silence:** Who will crack first

2.6 Negotiation Objectives

1. To obtain a fair and reasonable price consistent with the project objectives
2. To develop and maintain a good and sustainable relationship with the supplier

2.7 The 3 Requirements for a Contract

1) Offer and acceptance
One party makes an offer that the other accepts

2) Consideration
Something of value (the Consideration) must be exchanged

3) There must be an intention by both parties to be **legally bound** and persons entering into a contract must have **legal capacity**

It is not possible to have a legally binding contract for an illegal activity.
Contracts do not have to be written. Verbal contracts if witnessed or recorded can be legally binding.
Anything said in a contract negotiation that influences the purchaser to accept the contract can be construed as part of the contract even if not included in the contract document.

2.8 Meanings of Contract Terms

Standard Contracts

Drafting contracts is an expensive and time consuming business. It is always better to use a standard contract wherever possible at least as a starting point for negotiation.

Some of the principal points that should be covered in a standard contract are as follows:-
(Based primarily on PMI Monograph "Contract Administration for the Project Manager")

Changes

Changes to project scope are a major area of cost growth. All contracts should define the process by which any changes to the contract (project) can be accommodated and should include the paperwork, tracking systems, and approvals necessary for authorising changes.

Change is inevitable and should be viewed as an opportunity.

Warranties

- Express warranty: Contract explicitly states what the level of quality should be.
- Implied warranty: Concerns "merchantability" or fitness of use".

Applies where the seller knows the purpose of the goods and the buyer is relying on the seller's judgement. However if the client is as "expert" and relies on his own skill and judgement then there is no implied warranty. If the goods are to the specification drawn up by the buyer or as agreed by an "expert" buyer then unfitness for use is not the responsibility of the supplier.

A warranty is for a specified period of time which in most countries also has a legal minimum. The main purpose of a warranty is to instil confidence in potential purchasers.

Doctrine of waiver

It is important that any breach of contract by the other party is formally brought to their attention even if the prescribed remedy is not enforced. This is because, under the Doctrine of Waiver, failure to do can cause the relinquishing (waiving) of contractual rights.

Bonds

A bond is a guaranteed payment to subcontractors by the prime or the guarantor. It is a promise to pay a certain sum of money if a stated condition is not fulfilled.

The two more common types are.

1. Performance Bond

Here, for a fee, a third party, usually a bank or insurance company would guarantee to the client the due performance of the contract. If the contractor defaults the client can demand the value of the bond from the third party.

2. Payment bond.

This is similar except that the bond guarantees payments to the subcontractors by the Prime via the guarantor.

Breach

- *Breach of Contract* is the failure by either party to perform a contractual obligation
- *Damages* can be claimed equal to the loss sustained.
- *Material Breach* (sometimes called a *Repudiatory* breach or *Fundamental* breach) is more serious than a simple contract breach. In this case the innocent party is discharged from any further obligations under the contract and can claim Liquidated Damages. (See below)

Time is of the essence

When "*time is of the essence*" is stipulated then late delivery is a *material breach*.

Liquidated Damages

A Breach may give rise to a claim for Liquidated Damages. Liquidated damages are a form of compensation and are not meant to be punitive. They are pre-determined in the contract and should be a fair assessment of the damage suffered. They are sometimes referred to as **Compensatory** damages.

Consequential Loss

Consequential Loss represents indirect losses incurred as a result of a Breach. For example an airline booking system fails to work and as a consequence a flight takes of empty and all the revenue is lost. Most companies will not accept consequential loss agreements or if they do are strictly limited.

Force Majeure

An act of God. An event that could not reasonably have been guarded against.

Acceptance Criteria

The list of contractual conditions which when complied with will allow acceptance and contract closure.

Non disclosure agreement

This is a legal contract between you and another party in which you agree to share information with them and they agree not to disclose that information to anyone else. Breaking this agreement could lead to substantial damages

2.9 Letter of Intent

The phrase "letter of intent" has no legal meaning. Generally speaking a letter of intent does not intend to give rise to any legal obligation. However if a letter makes it clear that it a prospective purchaser expects the seller to act as if it were a purchase order then simply using the description "letter of intent" will not be a defence in law.

2.10 Privity of Contract

When contracts are in place between buyer and the prime contractor and between the prime and sub-contractors, Privity of Contract is a legal term that recognises this and also that no contract exists between the buyer and the subcontractors, and that it is legally improper and unethical for a buyer to bypass a contractor and deal directly with a subcontractor without permission.

Beyond the legal issue, there are other reasons for a buyer to be cautious about dealing with subcontractors. In doing so, the buyer may inadvertently relieve the prime contractor of certain responsibilities. For example, if a buyer informs a subcontractor that things might work better if the subcontractor would "try the following approach." and the subcontractor runs into trouble, the prime contractor may rightfully claim that the buyer's interference caused the problems.

Because there is no contract between the Buyer and the Sub-contractor the Buyer has no remedy. against the subcontractor for poor work in the event of the Prime going into liquidation. Because of this some Buyers will require direct contracts with subs regarding quality of work.

2.11 Disputes

Disputes between parties to a contract are almost inevitable. It is therefore essential that the contract defines a process by means of which disagreements are resolved so as to facilitate a speedy resolution.

Step 3: Administer Procurement

Contract administration is the process of ensuring that the seller's performance meets the contractual requirements. The project manager is responsible for monitoring the vendor's performance against the contract's specifications and performance standards.

3.1 Managing Suppliers

Poor performance of suppliers is a major cause of project problems. You must agree with your suppliers the means by which you will actively manage them. This is especially important when you believe your project may not be high on their list of priorities.

Particular attention should be paid to the following:

- How changes to the contract will be managed
- How supplier performance will be measured and managed
- Arrangements for inspections and audits
- Payment arrangements
- How you will deal with disputes and claims
- How you will record and manage contract information

3.2 Further Contractual Considerations

- When selecting suppliers ensure that they have a quality system and are applying it. e.g ask to see recent audit reports
- Enter into a contract type appropriate to what is being purchased
- Have a contract that encourages quality behaviour. e.g penalties for late or poor delivery and incentives for good performance
- Make sure both you and the supplier fully understand the nature of the contract and the deliverables
- Try and ensure that the relationship is mutually beneficial
- Try to tie payments to targeted benefits not just delivery of boxes or commodities
- Review the product and supplier's performance regularly
- Conduct regular random inspections of the supplied goods/services during the term of the arrangement;
- Continuously monitor performance. e.g Have regular progress meetings and keep statistics of quality and timeliness of deliverables
- Check that all conditions and clauses are acted upon - be aware of breaches and know how to deal with them - and take action if non-conformance occurs;
- Keep your suppliers aware of any changed requirements. e.g make sure your change control system includes your suppliers.
- Seek legal advice if there has been any breaches of contract;
- Advise the supplier in writing if not satisfied with any aspect of their performance or product;
- Act immediately if a problem occurs and not wait until it gets out of hand.

Step 4: Close Procurement

The input to this process is all the contract documentation starting with the original contract and including all documents generated during the life of the contract. The output is a closed contract file for archiving including statements of formal acceptance and closure of the contract.

Contract close-out has two main elements:-

1) Product Verification

Has all the contracted work been carried out and accepted by the customer?

2) Administrative Close-out

All contract records must be updated and place in the contract file, which should be part of the complete project file. Proper closeout of contract documentation is also important should a *Procurement Audit* be carried out. As well as ensuring that all proper procedures have been adhered to the main purpose of the audit is to identify successes and failures that can improve future contracts.

Procurement Management Practice Questions

1. Breach of contract is a failure to perform a contractual obligation. A material breach is a form of breach. Which statement best defines or describes a material breach?

a. The focus of the breach is on the materials delivered or not delivered.
b. It is less severe than simple breach.
c. The non faulted party (the one who did not cause the breach) is discharged from any further obligation.
d. This only applies to the contractor's material supplies

2. Of the contract types listed below, which one places the greatest degree of risk on the buyer?

a. Cost-plus-percentage fee
b. Cost-sharing
c. Cost-plus-fixed fee
d. Cost-plus-incentive fee

3. Under which of the following is it possible for a party to relinquish rights he or she has under the contract.

a. Quantum meruit
b. Assignment of claims
c. Material breach
d. Doctrine of Waiver

4. A legally binding contract that is offered unilaterally is :

a. purchase order
b. work statement
c. invitation to tender
d. warranty

5. Which of the following will best ease the workload and increase the probability of winning contracts?

a. Early appointment of the proposal manager
b. Early identification of the proposal staff
c. Using standard scopes of services language
d. All of the above

6. From the contractor's (seller's) perspective, "liquidated damages" is a form of which kind of incentive?

a. Positive
b. Negative
c. Nominal
d. Reverse

7. The four steps of Procurement Management are:

a. Plan Procurement, Conduct Procurement, Administer Procurement, Contract Closeout
b. Plan Procurement, Conduct Procurement, Administer Procurement, Close Procurement
c. Planning, Procurement, Administration, Closeout
d. Procurement Planning, Source Selection, Contract Administration, Contract Closure

8. Force majeure is a term derived from insurance law meaning—

a. Superior or irresistible force, such as lightning, earthquakes, storms, or floods
b. Any party to a contract can redress alleged illegalities through any U.S. District Court
c. The buyer can seek damages from the seller due to major contract breaches
d. The seller neglected to exercise due care in performance and is thus subject to a breach of contract action

9. Incentive clauses in a contract are designed primarily to:-

a. Increase cost to the buyer
b. Give an increased profit potential to the seller
c. Reduce buyer risk
d. To align the seller's goals in line with those of the buyer.

10. Why is it important to have a disputes clause in a contract defining the procedures to be used to resolve problems?

a. Having a defined process will facilitate the resolution of disputes as soon as possible
b. The tracking of claims is important in case of subsequent litigation
c. Disputes can be brought before an Arbitration Board for resolution only when the formal procedure has been followed
d. There may be an adverse relationship formed without such a procedure

11. Which of the following is usually the best strategy when creating a contract?

a. Prepare a unique contract
b. Tailor an existing contract
c. Use standard clauses in contract
d. Use a mix of standard and specially written clauses

12. A purchase order becomes a legally binding contract when—

I.   It is issued by the buyer
II.   It is received by the vendor.
III.   The vendor initiates work on the purchase order.
IV.   It is accepted and signed by the vendor.
a.   I
b.   II and/or III
c.   III
d.   III or IV

13. Which of the following is not an appropriate response to a breach?

a.   Liquidated damages
b.   Punitive damages
c.   Compensatory damages
d.   Consequential damages

14. Monitoring of Sub Contractors is best done by using:

a.   Agreed measures and procedures
b.   Weekly meetings
c.   Work completed reports
d.   WBS

15. Which is not a negotiation tactic.

a.   Imposing deadlines
b.   Person with authority is absent
c.   Budget limit
d.   All are negotiating tactics

16. Which of the following payments are Payment bonds specifically designed for?

a.   Insurance premiums
b.   Weekly payrolls
c.   Incremental earned value charges
d.   Subcontractors, labourers, and materials

17.   What do you call a situation when a contractor fails or refuses to complete the contractual conditions?

a.   Breach
b.   Cessation of work
c.   Flawed contract
d.   Delay

18. In a situation where a professional contract administrator is assigned to the project then a project manager __

a. Does not need to actively manage the contract
b. Can delegate all responsibility to the contract administrator
c. Must still manage all major aspects of the contract
d. Does not need to be familiar with the small print of the contract

19. A bilateral contract can arise from:

a. Request for Quotation
b. Request for Proposal
c. Invitation to bid
d. All of the above

20. Final contract negotiations are completed in which contract step?

a. Administer Procurements
b. Source Selection
c. Conduct Procurements
d. Contract administration

21. Which item is not a basic requirement of a contract?

a. Offer
b. Acceptance
c. Consideration
d. Pricing structure

22. Requirements for formal acceptance and closure of the contract are usually defined in the

a. Proposal
b. Statement of work
c. Contract
d. Procurement audit report

23. Which term describes costs that would still exist even if the project terminated

a. Variable costs
b. Direct Costs
c. Indirect Costs
d. Sunk Costs

24. The legal contractual relationship that exists between the buyer and the seller is called—
a. Apparent authority
b. Contract privity
c. Terms and conditions
d. Force majeure

25. A purchase order is a good example of which form of contracting?

a. Unilateral
b. Bilateral
c. Trilateral
d. Informal

26. Which of the following activities is a key element of effective contract administration?

a. Holding a bidders conference
b. Establishing the appropriate contract type
c. Implementing a contract change control system
d. Developing the statement of work

27. Which of the following statements is not true with regard to cost reimbursement contracts?

a. The seller's interest in cost control diminishes.
b. The buyer is obliged to pay for all time booked at the agreed rate
c. The buyer's concern about the seller's performance increases.
d. The seller bears the greater financial risk.

28. What should be the objectives of a fair and ethical negotiation?

a. To obtain the best possible prices and terms for your organisation
b. To agree a price fair and reasonable to both parties
c. To develop and maintain a good relationship
d. Both b) and c)

29. The principal function of a warranty is to_

a. Provide assurance of the level of quality to be provided
b. Provide a way to assert claims for late payment
c. Provide a way to allow additional time following acceptance to correct deficiencies, without additional costs
d. Ensure that goods purchased fit the purposes for which they are to be used

30. Contract closeout and administrative closure are similar in that they both require—
a. That someone other than the project manager manage the activities involved
b. Verification that no errors occurred at any time while the work was being performed
c. That a WBS be prepared
d. Verification that the work was completed satisfactorily

31. Which of the following contract types places the greatest risk on the seller to control costs?

a. Fixed-price with economic price adjustment
b. Fixed-price incentive (firm target)
c. Firm-fixed-price
d. Cost-plus-award fee

32. Which of the following is the best definition of Liquidated Damages?

a. Compensation for losses incurred
b. Punishment for poor performance
c. Punishment for breach of contract
d. An incentive to perform

33. Which of the following does not represent a source of power in negotiation?

a. Being best prepared
b. Needing the business to meet business goals
c. Having alternative options
d. Having knowledge of the other persons situation

34. Which of the following contract types does not encourage the seller to control costs and, as a result, places the greatest risk on the buyer?

a. Cost-plus-award fee
b. Cost-plus-fixed fee
c. Cost-plus-incentive fee
d. Cost-plus-a-percentage-of-cost

35. Which of the following allows the innocent party to terminate the contract and claim damages?

a. Force Majeure
b. Doctrine of Waiver
c. Material Breach
d. Consequential Loss

36. The Cost Plus Percentage of Cost (CPPC) type of contract provides reimbursement of…..

a. Allowable costs plus an agreed fixed fee which is a percentage of the estimated cost as profit
b. Agreed fixed price for the delivered product plus a predetermined percentage fee for superior performance
c. Allowable cost of services performed plus an agreed upon percentage of the cost as profit
d. Agreed costs of time and consumables used

PRACTICE QUESTION ANSWERS

		Page	Paragraph	
1	C	209	2.8	
2	A	202	1.4	
3	D	208	2.8	
4	A	204	1.5	
5	D			Self evident
6	B	209	2.8	Liquidated damages are a cost to the seller if incurred thus they are a -ve incentive.
7	B	200		
8	A	208	2.8	
9	D	205	2	
10	A	210	2.1	
11	C	208	2.8	
12	D	204	1.5	
13	B	209	2.8	A Breach will give rise to compensation as defined in the contract but does not attract punitive damages.
14	A	210	3.1	
15	D	207	2.5	
16	D	208	2.8	
17	A	209	2.8	
18	C			Self evident
19	D	204	1.5	
20	C	200		
21	D	207	2.7	
22	C	209	2.8	
23	D	95	6.6	
24	B	209	2.10	
25	A	204	1.5	
26	C			a), b) and d) take place earlier in the procurement cycle.
27	D	203	1.4	
28	D	207	2.6	
29	A	208	2.8	
30	D	211	4	
31	C	204	1.4	
32	A	209	2.8	
33	B	206/7	2.4	You needing the business is a weakness if the other party Is aware of this.
34	D	203	1.4	
35	C	209	2.8	
36	C	203	1.4	

Chapter 11

Professional Responsibility

1 Professional Responsibility

What is professional responsibility? It can mean different things to different people. As a PMP, professional responsibility involves:

- Adhering to the PMP Code of Professional Conduct
- Maintaining high professional ethics
- Developing cultural competence in our emerging global society

How do we prepare for professional responsibility questions? What do we study? How can a multiple choice exam test ethics?

Professional responsibility questions typically pose an ethical, professional or cultural scenario and ask you to choose the best response. In most cases, the correct answer can be selected by simply asking yourself, "What is the *right* thing to do."

In short, most professional responsibility questions can be answered correctly by simply relying on your best common sense and a feel for what is morally right.

Your PMP exam will include eighteen questions testing your knowledge competency and judgment in the area of 'professional responsibility.' This represents a significant overall percentage of exam questions and actually serves as a benefit. For many candidates, professional responsibility questions are the easiest.

2 The PMI Code of Ethics & Professional Conduct

In the pursuit of the project management profession, it is vital that PMI members conduct their work in an ethical manner in order to earn and maintain the confidence of team members, colleagues, employees, employers, customers/clients, the public, and the global community. The PMP Code of Ethics and Professional Conduct is detailed in the Project Management Professional (PMP) Credential Handbook available for download at www.PMI.org. What follows in the next 4 paragraphs is based on the code but it is recommended that you download and study it as well as the material here.

3 Responsibility to the Profession

1. Be truthful at all times and in all situations
2. Report Code violations (with factual basis)
3. Disclose conflicts of interest
4. Comply with laws
5. Respect other's intellectual property rights
6. Support the Code

4 Responsibility to Customers and the Public

1. Be truthful at all times and in all situations
2. Maintain professional integrity (satisfy the scope of your professional services)
3. Respect the confidentiality of sensitive information
4. Refrain from gift or compensation giving/receiving where inappropriate
5. Ensure conflicts of interest do not interfere with client's interest or interfere with professional judgment.

5 Professional Competency

Professional people rendering a service have a duty to exercise reasonable care and to show such skill as can be reasonably expected of an ordinarily competent person exercising that particular profession. A client is not legally obliged to pay for work that is of inferior quality even if carried out under time and materials. Professional people also have obligations to customers and the wider community to provide goods and services that are fit for purpose and beyond moral reproach.

6 The Eight Ethical Principles

1. Honour
The principle of honour is to ensure that actions are beyond reproach, and that in turn demands total honesty from the professional.

2. Honesty
Actions must not violate any explicit or implicit agreement or trust.

3. Bias
The principle of bias focuses on ensuring decisions and actions avoid the possibility of conflicts of interest and eliminate bias in judgements

4. Professional adequacy
Professional adequacy is concerned with the ability of individuals to undertake allocated tasks. In other words is the person working within the limits of his/her capability?

5. Due care
Does the project follow appropriate quality assurance standards?

6. Fairness
Fairness focuses on ensuring all affected parties are considered in project deliberations. i.e. making sure all stake holder's views are considered.

7. Social Costs
This principle recognises that project staff should take professional responsibility and accountability for the social impacts of their projects.

8. Effective and efficient action
This is concerned with completing tasks and realising goals with the least possible expenditure of resources.

7 Ethnic and Cultural Norms

More and more projects are being carried out across international boundaries, and there is an increasing trend for project staff to work abroad. Ignorance of the culture worked in can cause conflict and offence where none was intended. Failure to identify cultural issues and take action can lead to culture shock. Often, the symptoms are ignored or simply not recognized.

PMI do not expect a knowledge of individual cultures, just an awareness that culture differences can cause problems, and a commonsense approach to avoiding them

In particular PMI expect you to have an awareness of Culture Shock

Symptoms of Culture Shock

- Productivity is negatively impacted
- Employees are disgruntled and frustrated
- People are unable to establish trust and good working relationships
- Productivity is negatively impacted
- Employees are disgruntled and frustrated
- Frequent miscommunication and misunderstandings
- Difficult to attract qualified and talented workforce

8 Stages of Culture Shock

- First stage incubation/honeymoon
    Everything is new and exciting
- Second stage - frustration in trying to adapt
    Feels impatient, frustrated, incompetent, angry
- Third stage - the turning point
    Gains understanding, feels positive OR returns home
- Fourth stage - integration
    Recognizes new culture has much to offer
- Fifth stage - re-entry shock
    Sometimes experiences difficulty returning to own culture

9 Dos and Don'ts in Managing Global Projects

In managing global projects, it is essential to develop cultural self-awareness. The first, and most important, step is becoming aware of your own cultural orientations and the impact they can make in managing projects across cultures.

You must prepare for cross-cultural project encounters with purpose and thoroughness. Here are a few dos and don'ts to consider ...

DO:

- Develop your cultural self-awareness.
- Set realistic expectations for yourself and others.
- Accept that you will make mistakes, but remain confident.
- Be patient.
- Slow down. Make relationships.
- Keep your sense of humour.
- Keep your integrity.
- Stay objective … minimize blame.

DON'T:

- Assume similarity.
- Try to adopt the orientations of the other culture. Adaptation does not mean adoption.
- Dwell on comparing the other culture with your own.
- Evaluate the other culture in terms of good or bad.
- Assume that just being yourself is enough to bring you cross-cultural success.

10. How to Develop Multicultural Excellence in Global Projects

As we rapidly evolve into a global community, many project managers find themselves managing project teams across vast geographical landscapes. To improve your success probability in such environments, it is essential to develop multicultural competencies.

Here are four things you can do to help develop multicultural excellence:

1.   **Multiple languages**.

Recruit core team members who speak multiple languages.

2.   **Multicultural experience.**

Provide core team members with multicultural experiences.

3.   **Cross-cultural experience**.

Arrange cross-cultural experiences for extended team members.

4.   **Continuous improvement.**

Acknowledge the continuous need to improve cross-cultural experiences for all team members.

11 Summary

1. Understand that perceptions and behaviours are different between cultures.

2. Be sensitive to and respect these differences.

3. Be fully truthful in all of your professional activities.

4. Maintain high integrity in all of your professional activities.

5. Follow through on your commitments.

6. Respond to ethical challenges by choosing to 'do the right thing.'

Notes on practice questions.

When answering questions on professional ethics you must strictly follow the code. You may not agree with all the answers. However the code of ethics says you must always do what is ethically correct regardless of personal or commercial considerations.

Professional Responsibility Practice Questions

1. While working on an external project your customer asks you to carry out some extra work that was not originally quoted for. Would you:

a. Honour the customer's request as sign of cooperation to ensure future business.
b. Refuse the request and report the customer to your sponsor
c. Acknowledge the request and advise the customer to submit a formal change request
d. Convene a meeting of the project team and rewrite the scope statement.

2. You are managing an internal R&D project. The initial test results are very poor and you believe management might cancel the project which would harm your career prospects. You should:

a. Recommend cancelling the project
b. Inform management about the results and wait for a response
c. Inform management and recommend repeating the tests
d. Say nothing until you perform additional tests to verify the initial results

3. During an informal meeting with your project client you are offered a bribe to change the product to meet a specific need. This will result in additional project costs.

Would you:

a. Turn down the offer and inform your sponsor.
b. Accept the offer and issue a change order
c. Ask for time to make a more detailed investigation.
d. Do nothing until you have made sure that you can protect yourself from any legal liabilities.

4. As the project manager for a government project you are asked to approve a press release. Upon reading it you identify some misleading statements in the release.

Would you:

a. Inform the project sponsor of the discrepancy and refuse to approve the release
b. Approve the release but send a memo to the sponsor advising that you are aware of the discrepancy and will refer any questions your receive to the sponsor
c. Completely rewrite the press release and include the correct information
d. Approve the release as requested

5. Your project is running out of cash and significant work remains. You are directed by senior management to instruct your people to use another project's charge numbers while working on your project. You should:

a. Follow instructions
b. Inform the corporate auditors
c. Understand the background of management's instructions before taking any action
d. Shut down the project, if possible

6. While reviewing the estimates from the functional managers assigned to your project you discover that one cost estimate is clearly higher than those submitted for previous projects. You should:

a. Reject the estimate and remove the functional manager from the project
b. Request the supporting details for the estimate to ensure it has been properly prepared.
c. Accept the estimate and plan to use the additional funding as a reserve.
d. Question each functional manager for information about this estimate.

7. You are working in a country where it is customary to exchange gifts between contractor and customer. Your company code of conduct clearly states that you cannot accept gifts from any client. Failure to accept the gift from this client may cause grave offence. Would you:

a. Provide the customer with a copy of your company code of conduct and refuse the gifts.
b. Exchange gifts with the customer and keep the exchange confidential
c. Contact your project sponsor and /or your legal or public relations group for assistance.
d. Ask the project sponsor or project executive to exchange gifts.

8. You recruit a new team member from a competitor and she offers to share confidential information from his previous company regarding a contract you are both bidding for. You should:

a. Accept the information and agree to keep it confidential between you and the new hire.
b. Advise her that you do not want the information
c. Review the information and only accept only what may have a direct impact on the bid.
d. Ignore the offer.

9. You are asked to write a paper for your sponsor to present at a convention. You are told that you will not be acknowledged as the author of the paper. You should:

a. Go along with the request.
b. Demand that your name also appears
c. Refuse to follow the instructions
d. Go over the head of your sponsor seeking advice

10. An example of a conflict of interest would be:

a. As a public official you make a decision about a contract award that will benefit you personally
b. You and a functional manager disagree with a task cost estimate
c. Your sponsor decides to cancel your project because it no longer supports the company strategy
d. Your personality conflicts with that of a key member of your project team.

11. Each of the following describes the use of an ethical approach except:

a. Attempting to understand the religious and cultural sensitivities of the country in which you have been assigned.
b. Ensuring that personal interest does not interfere with your decision making process.
c. Accepting gifts in exchange for favouring one contractor over another
d. Maintaining confidentiality of sensitive information obtained during the project life cycle.

12. To maintain the customer's schedule, massive overtime will be required between Christmas and New Years. Many of your team members have put in for vacation during this time. You should:

a. Let the schedule slip and inform the customer
b. First give the employees the choice of working overtime
c. Make the employees cancel their vacation plans and work overtime
d. Hire temporary employees for the overtime

13. Which of the following situations describes a violation of the PMP® Professional Code of Conduct?

a. Accepting a gift that is within the customary guidelines of the country or province you are currently working in.
b. Use of confidential information to advance your position or influence a critical decision.
c. Complying with laws and regulations of the state or province in which project management services are provided
d. Disclosing information to a customer about a situation that may have an appearance of impropriety.

14. In order to balance the needs of the many stakeholders involved in your project the most desirable method to achieve resolution of conflicts would be:

a. Compromise
b. Forcing
c. Controlling
d. Confrontation

15. In a project to produce a consumer product you agree a test specification with the client. Your sponsor thinks the tests are too severe and instructs you to change them without informing the customer.

a. Use the customer's test specification.
b. Use the modified test specification without telling the customer
c. Use the modified test specification and inform the customer
d. Tell your sponsor that you want to set up a meeting with the customer to resolve the conflict

16. In order for the project manager to fully and effectively understand a stake holder's personal concerns or grievances it may necessary to:

a. Ask for a written description of the problem and submit it through the project office
b. Schedule a project review session with the entire project team
c. Attempt to empathize with the stakeholder
d. Involve the project sponsor as an arbitrator

17. As a project manager what should you do if you discover weaknesses or development needs in your project team?

a. Remove any team members who have demonstrated weaknesses in critical knowledge areas
b. Communicate those weaknesses and establish a performance improvement program
c. Hire additional resources to compensate for weak areas
d. Wait for the team members to fail in an assignment to justify termination.

18. You have just changed jobs and discovered that your new employer routinely violates health and safety regulations. You should:

a. Do nothing; it's not your problem
b. Start by asking management if they are aware that regulations are being violated
c. Talk to the corporate legal department
d. Inform the appropriate government agencies about the violations

19. A key responsibility of the project manager is to ensure that project stakeholders receive regular communication. As part of this process the project manager should attempt to:

a. Determine the specific needs of individual stakeholders before communicating information
b.   Communicate only with those stakeholders who approve of the project.
c. Filter the information to remove any awkward facts.
d. Restrict information to specific technical details

20. What is the best method of developing an effective means of communication for your project stakeholders?

a.   Discuss the available options with the stakeholders and obtain their input
b.   Use the standard arrangements that have been used for your previous projects
c.   Use multiple forms of communication to make sure everyone receives the information
d.   Develop a project specific communications infrastructure.

21. One of your matrix team member is due for promotion which you agree is merited. If granted, the employee will be reassigned elsewhere causing a problem for your project. You should:

a.   Support the promotion but work with the employee and the employee's new management to develop a good transition plan
b.   Ask the employee to refuse the promotion until your project is completed.
c.   Arrange to delay the promotion until the project is completed
d.   Tell the employee that it is his responsibility to find a suitable replacement so that the project will not suffer.

22. One of your senior stakeholders is using personal power to change the scope of an agreed upon deliverable. You should:

a.   Refer the stakeholder to the change control process
b.   Agree to the change because the stakeholder is too powerful to resist.
c.   Contact the legal department and suspend all further project work
d.   Assess the impact of the change before taking any action.

23. You disagree with the client as to the value of completed work under contract. The project manager should:

a.   Ignore the customer concerns and process the invoices
b.   Document the dispute and refer to the provisions of the contract that address interpretations and disputes
c.   Advise the customer that ambiguous information in contracts should be interpreted in favour of the contractor
d.   Amend the contract in your favour

24. Your sponsor has given you a cash bonus to be disbursed among your team members. One of them has performed poorly on your project. You should:

a.   Provide everyone with an equal share
b.   Provide everyone a share based upon their performance
c.   Ask the workers to decide among themselves how the bonus should be subdivided
d.   Ask the sponsor to make the decision

25. Before reporting a perceived violation of an established rule or policy the project manager should

a. Determine the risks associated with the violation
b. Ensure there is a reasonably clear and factual basis for reporting the violation
c. Ignore the violation until it actually affects the project results
d. Convene a committee to review the violation and determine the appropriate response

26. Project Managers can contribute to their organization's knowledge base and to the profession of project management most effectively by:

a. Developing and implementing a project review and lessons learned process
b. Establishing strict guidelines for protecting intellectual property
c. Promote the use of ad hoc project management
d. Ensuring that all project plans are developed before the project team is formed

27. You have been assigned two concurrent projects. Because of the nature of the projects, you have a conflict of interest. You should:

a. Do the best you can and tell no one
b. Ask to be removed from one of the projects
c. Ask to be removed from both of the projects
d. Inform your sponsor and ask for his advice

28. Upon routine testing of one of the intermediate product deliverables of your project you find that it is slightly out of specification. You believe it will not affect final product quality. You should:

a. Accept the product
b. Document the test result and ask the contractor to find a solution
c. Reject the product outright
d. Allow the lower standard this time but inform the contractor he must meet the specification in future

29. An effective method for improving an organization's project management knowledge base is through:

a. Coaching and mentoring
b. Referent power
c. A weak Matrix organizational structure
d. Fast Tracking

30 You have managed the construction of an effluent treatment plant. You learn that there is a very slight risk of polluting the local water supply under conditions of exceptionally high throughput, which could cause slight stomach problems to anyone drinking the water

As project manager, you should

a. Order a detailed examination to determine the extent to which the problem exists and keep the public fully informed of the situation.
b. Do nothing because the risk is very low
c. Tell the public there is no problem.
d. Advise the public not to use the water for drinking until further notice.

31 An organization has recently started outsourcing work to a low cost, high value, engineering centre located in a different country. Which of the following should the project manager provide for the team as a proactive measure?

a. A training course on the laws of the country
b. A course on linguistic differences
c. An exposure to the cultural differences
d. A communication management plan

32 An organization is certified to a stringent environmental standard and uses that as the key differentiator with its competitors. Alternative identification during scope planning for a particular project has thrown up an approach that involves a risk of environmental contamination. The team evaluates that the likelihood of the risk is very low. What should the project team do?

a. Drop the alternative approach
b. Work out a mitigation plan
c. Procure an insurance against the risk
d. Plan all precautions to avoid the risk

33. Which of the following statements concerning cross-cultural differences is true?

a. There is no one "best way" for project organization.
b. Some cultures have values, some not.
c. Cultural dilemmas should be denied so as not to allow them to disrupt project work.
d. You should not let concern for other peoples cultural beliefs get in the way of the project.

34 One of your project team members has a broad regional accent. Two other members of your team are constantly joking and commenting on his accent. What is the best way to handle the situation?

a. Just ignore it so as not to make things worse by drawing attention to it.

b. Conduct a team training session on ethical and cultural considerations

c. Take the two members aside and tell them to modify their behaviour

d. Ask the HR manager to intervene.

35 You wish to reward a team member. She knows there is no money in the budget for a bonus so she asks if you can give her a few days off and call it sick leave. What do you do?

a. Say yes because Hygiene theory states that she needs motivators to keep performing

b. Say yes because Expectancy theory states that people expect to be rewarded for good performance

c. Just say no because that would be unethical

d. Say no but assure her that you will try and find some way to reward her in the future.

36 You have prepared an ITT for a construction project. Your brother in law calls you and says he intends to bid for the project. You know he is capable of doing a good job. What should you do?

a. Tell your brother in law not to bid as it would cause you a conflict of interest.

b. Disclose your conflict of interest then use your normal selection criteria

c. Disclose your conflict of interest then absent yourself from the selection process

d. Do nothing and follow your normal selection process

PRACTICE QUESTION ANSWERS

1	C	Increase in scope must always be subject to the formal process
2	D	There is no point in causing alarm until the original results have been verified
3	A	You should report any bribery attempt without delay.
4	A	You cannot approve a misleading release so you must escalate the issue,
5	C	This seems like the wrong thing to do but before taking drastic action you should get more information
6	B	Once again discover the facts before taking action
7	C	Whatever you do here could cause difficulties so escalate the problem to your sponsor
8	B	It would be unethical to make use of this information so you must ignore it.
9	B	Your sponsor is trying to act dishonestly. The ethically correct thing is to insist you are credited.
10	A	The personal benefit means there is a conflict of interest
11	C	C is clearly unethical
12	B	C is unacceptable and A and C are ethically acceptable but B should be tried first
13	B	B is clearly unethical
14	D	As we have learned earlier, confrontation is the best way of resolving conflict.
15	D	It would be unethical to do anything without involving the customer
16	C	If one of your stakeholders has personal concerns you should first discuss the situation with them.
17	B	Part of your job is to mentor your team so you must help them to improve their performance.
18	B	You cannot ignore this but you must give the management an opportunity to correct things.
19	A	You must report the truth but not every stakeholder needs to know everything.
20	A	As communication is a two way process you should agree methods and frequency with your stakeholders.
21	A	Ethically you must support the promotion and manage whatever problems it causes you.
22	A	No one can be allowed to bypass the formal process no matter how senior.
23	B	You must follow the formal contractual process.
24	B	It is your responsibility and A would be taking the easy way out and would demotivate your best staff.
25	B	You must act but gather information before you do so
26	A	Clearly the best answer.
27	D	You must always declare a conflict of interest but take advice from your sponsor.
28	D	As quality will not be affected rejection would be too drastic but you should insist on the correct quality in future
29	A	Giving your team the benefit of your experience is an ethical approach as it benefits everyone.
30	A	You cannot lie or do nothing but because the risk is low you should give the public information to enable them to make their own decisions.
31	C	In order to avoid misunderstandings the project team need to be aware of cultural differences.
32	A	You probably won the project on your environmental approach. It would be wrong to compromise that.
33	A	B is false and C and D are unethical. You must always try and allow for cultural differences.
34	C	You do not want to draw attention to the problem but you cannot ignore it. A quiet word is best.
35	D	Saying yes would be unethical but an outright no would be demotivating.
36	C	All approaches are possible but C would prevent any accusation of conflict of interest.

Notes

Notes

Printed in Great Britain
by Amazon.co.uk, Ltd.,
Marston Gate.